Finally, a book that can guide us men into becoming what we have long pretended to be—wildly good lovers! This book is radically helpful on the journey toward becoming sexually healthy and fully embodied. Sheila and Keith have written a must-read for anyone who has previously had sex, is currently having sex, or would like to have sex in the future! Thank you for this wise guide.

Andrew J. Bauman, author of *The Sexually Healthy Man* and founder and director of the Christian Counseling Center: For Sexual Health & Trauma

I've worked with thousands of husbands, and this book answers many of the questions they've asked about how to have great sex. If you want intimate connection and also want research-based answers, do your marriage a favor and get this book.

Adam King, MA, marriage coach and cofounder of Dear Young Married Couple

The Good Guy's Guide to Great Sex is a life (in the bedroom) changing resource to help couples close the gap between what they hope for from sex and what they actually experience. Written by a bestselling sex expert and her physician husband, this hope-infused, medically savvy book will empower men to love their wives as equal partners in all things amorous, as well as help them understand what's really going on between the sheets of sexual passion and sexual struggle. Here you'll find fresh perspective and compelling rationale for why so much of what we've been taught about sex is as unhealthy as it is unhelpful. This book may make you mad (when you realize you've been misled), but it will bring you joy. It may make you blush, but it will heal your shame. And best of all, it will deepen your marital intimacy at every level—emotional, spiritual, and physical.

Michael John Cusick, author of *Surfing for God*

Many men receive unhelpful messages about their sexuality, and few are taught how to build a great sex life. This book changes all that! I hope the principles taught in *The Good Guy's Guide to Great Sex* become the new standard for faith-based sex education in the home.

Dan Purcell, founder of Get Your Marriage On!

Most married couples that are disconnected and hurting sexually lack the tools and the language to process what is going on and the guidance to know what they can do about it. Not anymore.

Neil Josephson, national director of FamilyLife Canada

This is a desperately needed book and one I wish I had twenty-five years ago! The authors skillfully connect the emotional, spiritual, theological, and physical aspects of sexuality, all in layman's terms. For guys who want to love their wives well, this book lays the foundation for a lifetime of growth together in love, mutual joy, and intimate connection. I will be passing it out in all my marriage counseling.

Sam Powell, pastor of First Reformed Church, Yuba City, California

Finally, a feminist sex book for Christian men, by a man! Keith's clear and accessible language pushes against the prevailing culture of male-centric sexual advice, creating something that is mutually edifying precisely because it is female-forward. Packed with the latest psychological, physiological, and sociological research, it's not just a good sex book, it demonstrates a more holistic way to be a man and a husband. I highly recommend it!

Jonathan Puddle, pastor and author of *You Are Enough*

Sheila Gregoire knocks it out of the park again with her new book *The Good Guy's Guide to Great Sex*. This book offers a straightforward, no-nonsense approach to addressing the issues of male sexual frustration and dysfunction often present in today's marriages. Simple and practical yet theologically grounded, Sheila's message doesn't back down from the realities of today's marital landscape, challenging her readers to rediscover the true meaning of sex along with a path back to sexual enjoyment and greater intimacy.

Carl Thomas, CEO of XXXchurch and founder of Live Free Ministries

The Gregoires are helping us develop a better, more biblical understanding of sex and sexuality. This book will not only challenge your paradigms but also greatly improve your sex life! Find out how you can rethink sex to revitalize your sexual intimacy. I highly recommend this book for all couples who want to experience healthy sexuality in the bedroom—and beyond!

Nick Stumbo, MDiv, executive director of Pure Desire Ministries

The

GOOD GUY'S
GUIDE TO
GREAT SEX

The

GOOD GUY'S GUIDE TO GREAT SEX

Because *Good Guys* Make the *Best Lovers*

SHEILA WRAY GREGOIRE
AND DR. KEITH GREGOIRE

ZONDERVAN
BOOKS

ZONDERVAN BOOKS

The Good Guy's Guide to Great Sex
Copyright © 2022 by Sheila and Keith Gregoire

Requests for information should be addressed to:
Zondervan, *3900 Sparks Dr. SE, Grand Rapids, Michigan 49546*

Zondervan titles may be purchased in bulk for educational, business, fundraising, or sales promotional use. For information, please email SpecialMarkets@Zondervan.com.

ISBN 978-0-310-36176-3 (audio)

Library of Congress Cataloging-in-Publication Data

Names: Gregoire, Sheila Wray, 1970- author. | Gregoire, Keith, 1969- author.
Title: The good guy's guide to great sex : because good guys make the best lovers / Sheila Wray Gregoire, Keith Gregoire.
Description: Grand Rapids : Zondervan, 2022. | Includes bibliographical references. | Summary: "A candid companion to the bestselling guide for women, The Good Guy's Guide to Great Sex gives you suggestions for a fulfilling sex life for both you and your wife, whether you're just starting out or simply want to make your sex life what you've always hoped it would be and aren't sure how to get there"—Provided by publisher.
Identifiers: LCCN 2021039684 (print) | LCCN 2021039685 (ebook) | ISBN 9780310361749 (trade paperback) | ISBN 9780310361756 (ebook)
Subjects: LCSH: Sex counseling. | Sex—Religious aspects—Christianity. | Men—Sexual behavior.
Classification: LCC HQ28 .G74 2022 (print) | LCC HQ28 (ebook) | DDC 306.70811—dc23/eng/20211202
LC record available at https://lccn.loc.gov/2021039684
LC ebook record available at https://lccn.loc.gov/2021039685

To Connor and David,
two of the best guys we
know. We're so grateful
you're in our family.

Contents

Part 1: Up Close and Personal (All about Sex)

1. What Is Great Sex?...1
2. Let's Get Medical (How Sex Works) 11
3. Let's Get Frisky! The Sexual Response Cycle..............24

Part 2: The Three Components of Great Sex

Physical Pleasure

4. Mind the Gap!...41
5. Going Back to Square One...............................50
6. Ladies First (All about Orgasm) 58
7. When Sex Isn't Working..................................75

Emotional Companionship and Closeness

8. The Greatest Need......................................89
9. Sex Sorta Begins in the Kitchen (But Not Why You Think) .. 100
10. Let's Get Romantic 110

Spiritual Intimacy and Oneness

11. Making Love, Not Just Having Sex 121
12. When Sex Seems Ugly................................128
13. Is Sex a Need?....................................136
14. You Don't Need That Fix............................147
15. Beyond Bouncing Your Eyes.........................163
16. Adding Some Spice 174

Part 3: Putting It All Together

17. When You Want More...............................187
    Final Thoughts: The Truck Stop and
    the Five-Star Restaurant............................202

    Appendix 1: Getting Ready for the Honeymoon 205
    Appendix 2: Discussion Questions 221
    Acknowledgments 227
    Notes 231

Part 1

UP CLOSE AND PERSONAL (ALL ABOUT SEX)

CHAPTER 1

What Is Great Sex?

When raccoons try to eat cotton candy, the result is both hilarious and sad—as a quick search on YouTube will show. Raccoons, by instinct, wash their food before they eat it. What happens when a raccoon gets a hold of cotton candy, then? He dutifully submerges it, and it dissolves instantly, leaving the desperate animal frantically searching for his disappearing meal. The poor creature did exactly what he had been wired to do, and it turned out all wrong.

Sometimes sex works that way too. We treat sex as we've been programmed to—by our culture, by pornography, by our church—and that method for finding sexual fulfillment leaves us empty-handed. And often our unrealistic, selfish, or otherwise distorted views of sex mean we don't only approach sex the wrong way, we also miss the point of what great sex is!

We want you to have great sex. We've been working for almost twenty years now to help couples achieve that, although we never dreamed when we first got married that's what we would be doing. One day back in 2004, Sheila came to me and said, "Hey, honey, wouldn't it be great to stand in front of thousands of people and talk about the most intimate details of our marriage?" Well, at least that's what I heard. She'd been on the phone that day with FamilyLife Canada, and they wanted to bring us on as speakers.

At first I wasn't enthusiastic about the idea. I mean, does

anybody really want to be marriage speakers? But I knew this was important to Sheila. Her writing and speaking career was taking off, and she needed more opportunities for big events. So I learned how to fasten lapel mics and use PowerPoint and tell stories of my unrealistic expectations when we got married. Interestingly, at almost every conference, we ended up being the ones roped into doing the sex talk because nobody else wanted to do it. I'm a doctor, so I guess they all figured I'd be comfortable with it. And Sheila? She can say "ejaculation" without batting an eye. So there we were, on stage in front of hundreds of couples, talking about sex.

Soon Sheila wrote even more books about sex. Her blog, *Bare Marriage*,[1] now focuses almost entirely on sex. Last year she and her blog team (including our oldest daughter) conducted the largest survey of Christian women's marital and sexual satisfaction that's ever been done. And they followed that with a men's survey that has formed the basis for this book.

We've overcome sexual difficulties in our own marriage. We've spoken about the struggle. And Sheila's blogged and written about it, mostly to women. Now we think it's time to talk to the guys and let you in on the route to great sex too.

What's the Definition of "Sex"?

If we're going to have great sex, we need to know what "great sex" means, as well as how to get there. This book is going to help with both. We will spend the first part looking at what great sex is and how our bodies were made to experience it. Then we'll spend the rest of the book talking about how to achieve it in our marriages and what to do when roadblocks pop up.

Let's start with something basic. What is sex?

That question may trigger flashbacks of "the talk" your parents clumsily gave you, but stay with us for a minute. When you hear, "What is sex?" you likely picture something specific. And chances are if you had to answer out loud, you'd probably hem and haw and try to figure out how to describe a guy's penis entering his wife's vagina and then try to find a polite way to talk about ejaculation.

Penis moving into vagina, a guy reaching climax—these are certainly a *part* of great sex. But they are only a part. If you treat sex as though the only point is for you to reach climax through intercourse, then your chances of experiencing great sex are likely to disappear, like that cotton candy in water. And if we think that is all great sex is, we are missing out on what God really meant for us.

This book was written nine years after Sheila published the women's version of this book—*The Good Girl's Guide to Great Sex*. That book was a "rah-rah" book that essentially said, *Sex is awesome, ladies! Sex is amazing! You can get there!* And sex—the way God intended it—is amazing. It is awesome. And your marriage *can* get there.

But here's the thing: as a guy, you likely already know that sex is amazing. You grew up hearing that men want and need sex. You likely don't need to be convinced that sex isn't shameful or dirty in the same way your wife—or future wife—may. (Though if you could use some convincing, some of those messages are on their way!) More importantly, the first time you have sex, it is likely to feel pretty good for you without a lot of coaching.

But for her? Maybe not so much.

In Sheila's original surveys for *The Good Girl's Guide to Great Sex*, she found that of couples who consummated their marriage on their wedding night, about 16 percent of women had awesome sex. For those few, the earth moved, the choir sang, and fireworks exploded like crazy. The rest? They felt pretty much nothing, except perhaps a lot of awkwardness and even a bit of (or a lot of) pain.

The *good* news is that if you follow the bottom 16 percent and the top 16 percent for ten years, they tend to end up in roughly the same place. Where you start out in your sex life doesn't matter nearly as much as what you do in the meantime. The *bad* news is that it often takes couples quite a few years to figure it all out.

We want to help with that. And that probably doesn't require us to give you a rah-rah message. You likely already feel excited and geared up to have a great time. But since sex is truly great only when it is great for both of you, what it does require is helping you figure out how to give your wife, or future wife, those same "let's get it on!" feelings.

Great Sex Means Prioritizing Her Experience

If what you're looking for is an amazing, passionate experience with a wife who is over-the-top excited and responsive, what you need is a manual on how to help *her* have great sex. This book is about helping both of you embrace sex in a way that helps her enjoy it and helps her want it as much as you. So she gets the rah-rah companion book, and you get the "here's how you can be her knight in shining armor" book—because you *can* be your wife's hero in the bedroom.

One more thing to clear up before we start: this book isn't a how-to manual to fix your wife so she sees sex the way you do. Yes, you may have an easier time wanting and enjoying sex than she does because of the messaging you were given growing up and because of basic anatomy (intercourse is pretty much automatically fun with a penis, but not necessarily so with a vagina). That does not mean you understand sex better than she does. Neither gender has the monopoly on messed up messages about sex, and neither gender is more innately primed for God's real version of intimacy. So if it tends to be easier for you to want and enjoy sex, that doesn't mean she is the problem you need to solve. Instead, we want to help you see how the narratives you've both been taught can make great sex as elusive as cotton candy in a river, and we want to give you a much better message. At the same time, you'll never have great sex unless she's able to embrace what God intended sex to be (hence the rah-rah)—which involves *you* embracing sex that way too.

What's Missing from Our Definition of Sex?

Okay, whew. With that big preamble, we'd like to revisit that first question about what sex is. To do that, we'd like you to do a thought experiment. Put yourself in your beloved's shoes, and think back to that stilted description of sex: "man puts penis into wife's vagina and moves around until he climaxes."

Do you see anything missing?

The woman's experience is absent. She's not doing anything—he's the one moving. She may not be enjoying it—he's the one climaxing.

Our everyday definition of sex, then, includes a guy's actions and a guy's pleasure, but pretty much leaves her as just a placeholder.

No woman wants to be a placeholder. Or a receptacle. Or an afterthought.

No woman wants her pleasure to be thought of as a "bonus" or an "extra."

And yet with the way we commonly define sex, that's exactly what happens.

If we're going to have great sex, the first thing we have to do is throw out our old definition of sex. Sex is not only intercourse, where he does something to her until he reaches climax. Sex encompasses *all sexual activity the two of you do together, with the aim of mutual satisfaction.* It's not only about intercourse, and it's not only about your climax. It's far more than that. It's meant to be *mutually* pleasurable.

Great Sex Is More Than Physical

That's a promising start, but we're *still* not at great sex. Why? Because great sex is not just about orgasm (even mutual ones!). Great sex is about orgasm as the result of, and natural culmination of, a vulnerable, intimate relationship. It's not just about a goal; it's about everything that leads up to it.

Genesis 4 gives us a hint of this more expansive definition of sex. I (Sheila) remember when I first heard the words of Genesis 4:1 spoken out loud. It was during a Sunday service in junior high when I was sandwiched into a wooden church pew with my friends. The pastor opened his imposing King James Version pulpit Bible and read, "And Adam knew Eve his wife; and she conceived . . ." We did what all junior high kids do when the topic of sex comes up in church. We giggled. A lot. Until our mothers gave us the look that causes you to sink down in the pew. But despite "the look," the giggling didn't subside because, come on, that's seriously funny. Adam "knew" his wife? It's as if God were embarrassed to use the real word or something!

But if you look at the Hebrew behind that word, you'll find something interesting. It's the same word that David used in the Psalms when he said, "Search me, God, and *know* my heart" (Psalm 139:23, emphasis added). It's a deep knowing, a deep longing for connection. Sex isn't just physical, it's also spiritual. It's about feeling closer than you ever thought possible to any other human being. It's intimacy. *And* it's orgasm. And somehow it all goes together!

Why Orgasm and Intimacy Are Linked

Not all orgasms result in intimacy, as the sex trafficking crisis, the pornography crisis, and the hooking-up culture tragically tell us. But we can see from how God made orgasm that intimacy was part of the design, even if we have since messed it up. One weekend marriage retreat, as we prepared to give our sex talk, Sheila remarked, "Remember to say *sex* and not just intimacy, okay?"

I thought she was reminding me to be more blunt, which, even though I'm a doctor, I sometimes do need reminding of. It can feel odd to stand up in front of hundreds of people and say words like *clitoris* or *ejaculation*. So if *intimacy* comes out of my mouth instead of *sex*, well, maybe I deserve a bit of a break.

But that wasn't it. Sheila was reminding me that too often we assume that sex and intimacy are the same thing, which may not be the case at all. Sheila and I believe that sex is an intrinsic and vital part of marriage. We believe that God designed it to be a marvelous expression of intimacy and a wonderful gift for both of us, which, miraculously, is also the way children are made. Unfortunately, that doesn't mean that sex is always intimate. Intimacy may be God's plan, but we can still miss the mark.

God made sex (and orgasm) so that it binds us together emotionally. We all produce a hormone called oxytocin, which is known as the "bonding hormone" because it does exactly that. Women produce oxytocin when they breastfeed their babies, which is why that experience increases bonding. Both men and women also make oxytocin when we orgasm. Oxytocin increases our feelings of connection to each other and is responsible (along with other hormones) for those pleasant feelings we associate with love.

Beyond that, orgasm takes us from the realm of thinking to that of experiencing, which requires vulnerability. Orgasm is unlikely to happen unless you can let go, which means it requires letting your guard down. You have to trust the other person if you are ever going to be able stop worrying about what you look like or what you're doing or whether you're quite proper. Once that happens, you can let go of control—and just *be*. But it takes vulnerability for a woman to open up and tell her husband what she likes and what makes her feel good. And it takes vulnerability for a man to try to pleasure her and admit that he doesn't know entirely what he's doing. Vulnerability, then, becomes the key to both orgasm and to intimacy—and that makes vulnerability the key to great sex!

Why Marriage Matters for Great Sex

Since vulnerability unlocks awesome sex, then when we take sex out of a committed relationship like marriage, sex loses something vital. When you're not truly committed to each other, you can't trust each other in the same way, and so you hit a vulnerability roadblock. Instead of being about bonding with another human being, sex can become self-focused, which makes sex less intense and less satisfying. Then, as with our desperate raccoon, people go looking for something that's missing. Sensing there's more to sex than what they are experiencing, they assume the way to get there is by pushing the physical boundaries, trying to increase their physical pleasure. That's why the whole world seems to be trying riskier and riskier things in bed and why things that would never have been talked about in polite company decades ago have now made it into sitcoms. And yet, though we push further and further, we still don't get that high because the high of sex isn't physical. It's emotional. It's relational. That's what turns mediocre sex into great sex.

As you read this book, you'll find it peppered with numbers and graphs. That's because in the year before we wrote this book, Sheila and her team surveyed twenty-five thousand men and women in four surveys looking at what makes great sex. Before we tell you all the fun stuff about orgasm that you likely want to hear, let us give you a far more foundational finding. One of the most striking correlations for sexual satisfaction in both men and women is reporting that they feel close to their spouse during sex. A woman who is satisfied with the intimacy of her sex life is five times more likely to reliably orgasm during sex. And a man who feels close to his wife during sex is 3.4 times more likely to report that his wife is an enthusiastic partner during sex. Feeling close to your spouse is a natural aphrodisiac!

Vulnerability, intimacy, orgasm—they're all designed to go together. That's what great sex is supposed to be, something that is at once physical, emotional, and spiritual. Emotional intimacy (trust and vulnerability), spiritual intimacy (feeling like you're one), and physical intimacy (the fireworks)—lose any one aspect, and you miss great sex entirely.

Our Story of Rather Terrible Sex

Now that we've defined great sex, and identified its key elements, we're ready to launch into how to find it! But one more quick thing before we continue. We want to "get real" for a moment. When we speak at marriage conferences, we always start the sex talk by saying, "We know what you're all thinking . . . *They must do it so well!* Whenever you meet people who write about sex or talk about sex, you assume they have it all together. But actually, this was the most difficult part of our marriage when we were first married. The reason we have anything to talk about at all is that we had so much to work through."

And it's true! People tend to write and speak in the areas of their lives that have been the biggest challenges. Without a challenge, you have nothing to learn—and thus nothing to share.

Trust us when we tell you that when we first married, sex was tough for us. For Sheila, it was awkward, and it hurt. Yet somehow that didn't stop me from wanting it all the time. And the more I wanted sex, the more Sheila felt that I loved her for what she could do for me, not that I really loved *her*. Of course, I didn't see it that way. I wanted sex *because* I loved her and wanted to share that experience with her.

I (Sheila) spent several years doing everything I could to "turn him off." I often tried to give a strong signal that "sex isn't going to happen tonight," even once we had worked through the pain issues and those were largely resolved.[2] One day I realized I was driving Keith away, which wasn't what I wanted. Around the same time, I read a magazine article by a woman who decided that she was never, ever going to say no to her husband in their marriage. When he wanted sex, she would be there for him. Having a type A competitive personality, I took it as a challenge. So without telling Keith, I decided to never, ever turn him down. And I kept a secret record by marking the days on a calendar.

But I (Keith) wasn't feeling any closer to her. I felt like something was missing. So with trepidation, I started a conversation. "I feel like we never make love." Sheila was incensed. How could I possibly feel that way when she was never saying no? She even pulled out that calendar with all those dates circled!

As we unpacked everything in that conversation, we made an important discovery. Great sex in our marriage wasn't just about Sheila not saying *no*. It was about getting Sheila to the point where she wanted to say *yes*. Sheila didn't really want a sexless marriage, and I certainly didn't want a sex life where my wife "did her duty." We both wanted to be swept away by passion.

We've spent the rest of our marriage trying to get there, and we've (mostly me!) learned a lot along the way. And Sheila finally figured out what all the fuss was about too. On that road we've had to do a lot of healing and a lot of forgiving. We've had to be more vulnerable with each other and more honest with ourselves.

And it's worth it.

We hope to take you on a journey in this book where sex changes from something that is far too simplistic to something that is the height of passion. That's what we think you really want. You don't want only orgasm. You want that closeness that comes from both of you deciding to be vulnerable and open with each other, focused on each other, and giving to each other. It's true intimacy at every level, not just physical.

That's real sex. That's great sex. Now let's get you there.

CHAPTER 2

Let's Get Medical (How Sex Works)

When I (Sheila) was young, I remember reading about sex from a book my mother gave me, with plump naked people holding hands and lying in bed. Apparently they moved around together until pressure built up like a sneeze, leading to some sort of explosion.

I had no idea why an explosive sneeze was supposed to feel good.

Fast-forward a few decades, and last year the two of us were talking with a man in his thirties who had heard us speak at a marriage conference. He told us about his wedding night, which came with a huge surprise. He knew what intercourse was, and he and his wife enjoyed it immensely. But afterward he was in for a shock when his erection disappeared. His whole life he had heard songs on the radio about going "all night long," and he wasn't prepared for needing time for his erection to build again.

Before we talk about how to achieve great sex, we want to make sure that you know enough about the mechanics of sex to avoid any similar misunderstandings! So consider this chapter the medical textbook part of the book. Let's start with some basic definitions.

Vagina: Part of the female genitals. It is the muscular tube that leads from the cervix (the lower end of the uterus, or womb) to the outside of the body.

Vulva: The "outside" part of the female genitals. It includes the opening to the vagina, the labia majora (bigger, outer lips), the labia minora (smaller, inner lips), and the clitoris.

Clitoris: A small bit of tissue near the top of the vulva, close to where the labia majora meet. It is very sensitive to stimulation and can become more so during sexual activity.

G-spot: A theoretical area of highly sensitive tissue along the front of the vaginal wall. Its existence is debated, but many women report that receiving stimulation on the front wall of the vagina (the side toward her belly button) is pleasurable.[1]

Erection: When the penis expands and becomes firm. This results from neurologic signals that allow for increased blood flow to the penis. Other parts of the body, such as the nipples and the clitoris, can also become "erect" when aroused.

Sperm: The man's reproductive cell. It combines with the woman's ovum (egg) at fertilization.

Semen: Sperm plus the fluid they are suspended in. Seminal vesicles and the prostate produce this fluid.

Prostate: A gland that surrounds the base of the urethra (urine tube) in men. It makes a fluid that mixes with sperm to form semen.

Ejaculation: The expulsion of semen from the penis at orgasm.[2]

Orgasm (or Climax): The peak of sexual excitement. It is accompanied by ejaculation in men and vaginal contractions in women. In both men and women, it is associated with intense pleasure. It is euphemistically called "coming."

Erogenous Zones: Parts of the body that respond to stimulation to produce positive sensations and sexual pleasure, typically the breasts and the genitals.

Intercourse: Sexual activity where the penis penetrates the vagina. This can be done in a variety of positions.

Refractory Period: The period of time after ejaculation when a man's erection diminishes and he is incapable of having a new one. This varies and tends to last longer as men age but is generally around thirty to sixty minutes.

Foreplay: Touching and stimulating parts of the body (including erogenous zones) to achieve arousal for both. Women who orgasm during intercourse usually do so only after a significant amount of foreplay.

Oral Sex: Stimulation of the genitals with the mouth and tongue. It is euphemistically called a "blow job" when performed on a man. The technical terms are fellatio when performed on a man, and cunnilingus when performed on a woman.

Manual Stimulation: Stimulation of the genitals with the hand and fingers. It is euphemistically called a "hand job" when performed on a man. Most women find it easier to become sexually aroused from manual stimulation or from oral stimulation than from intercourse.

Masturbation: Self-stimulation of the erogenous zones to bring oneself to orgasm. Men usually do this by rubbing the penis up and down. Women often rub the clitoris, insert something into the vagina, and/or rub their breasts. Masturbation is a sexual act designed to bring one to orgasm; merely touching one's genitals is not masturbation. A child rubbing his or her genitals is better described as "exploring" rather than masturbating in the sense we mean it in this book.

Let's Talk Reproduction

Before we get to how to make sex feel good, let's continue with the medical understanding of sex and tackle reproduction: how to get pregnant or how *not* to get pregnant (depending on your preference).

Here's how the whole baby thing works, barring any fertility issues: every menstrual cycle (approximately once a month), your wife's ovaries release an egg that travels down one of the fallopian tubes. This is called "ovulation." Most women don't feel this at all, although some can have some pain or cramping.[3] At ovulation, her hormone levels cause her libido to rise. Her body is ramped up to get pregnant, and she is more likely to say, "Let's get it on!" Her body then gets ready to be pregnant, thickening the lining of her uterus so that any fertilized egg can implant. The egg is viable for only a day or two. If the egg isn't fertilized and doesn't implant during that short window, it dies.

After ovulation, her hormone levels change, and her interest in sex often diminishes between ovulation and her period. This doesn't mean she can't enjoy sex, only that she may need more warming up. Then, roughly two weeks after ovulation—give or take a few days—if conception hasn't occurred, her body will shed the extra lining that has built up in the uterus, since it's not needed. That's her period, when she bleeds from her vagina, and it lasts roughly three to seven days. Women expel anywhere from one tea-spoon to five tablespoons of blood during their period (with 3–4 tbsp, or 45–60 mL, on average), and most women experience at least slight cramping, especially during the first one or two days. Many women experience much heavier cramping.

Now for your part in reproduction (which doesn't involve cramping—bonus!). When you orgasm, you ejaculate semen containing (on average) about one hundred million sperm per mL. Those sperm swim up the vagina, enter the uterus through the cervix, and try to meet up with the egg in the Fallopian tubes. If a sperm makes it that far, it joins with the egg (fertilization). The embryo then travels to the uterus where it hopefully implants, and if all goes well, it grows into a baby.

Your sperm can survive for up to five days while they "search" for the egg. That means that each cycle, your wife's fertility window lasts from about five days before ovulation to a couple of days after ovulation, for a total of about seven days, give or take a day or two. If you have sex before ovulation (if you are trying to get pregnant, perfect timing is a day or two before), those sperm will be hanging around, ready to meet the egg when it arrives. If you have sex after she's ovulated, your sperm may meet up with the egg while it is still viable.

If a woman has sex without any attempts to use birth control and has intercourse relatively frequently, her chance of getting pregnant in a year is about 85 percent. But what if she doesn't want to get pregnant?

Let's Talk Contraception

The decision about whether to use birth control (and what kind) can be challenging. Whatever you choose, make that decision together, taking account of each other's needs and wishes. Too often guys assume this is something "she will take care of." Don't be one of those guys. As a husband, you should share in the responsibility for the family-planning decisions you make as a couple, even if the method you decide on is predominantly or exclusively focused on her. Similarly, there are risks associated with some methods of birth control that one of you may have to take on. That should matter to you and should influence your decision. The one who has to bear the greater "costs" of the method should have the most say in what you choose.

A common reason for birth control failure is improper use. Picking a method with a lower effectiveness rate that you are more likely to perform 100 percent correctly is often better than picking one with a higher effectiveness rate that you are less likely to use perfectly. Talk to your physician about what is realistic for you. Also, some forms of birth control should not be used if you have certain health issues (for example, women with certain types of migraines should not use oral contraceptive pills). This chapter should not replace the advice of your healthcare provider. It is meant to guide you and help you to ask clarifying questions.

Natural Family Planning
HOW IT WORKS

Also called fertility awareness–based contraception, natural family planning involves keeping track of the wife's cycle and abstaining from intercourse at times when she is fertile. It works by ensuring that when her egg is present in the uterus, no sperm are there to fertilize it. Monitoring basal temperatures and checking cervical mucus can let you know more precisely when ovulation occurs. Many apps are available to help you do this.

PROS

In some religious traditions, sex is seen as a gift from God that gives the possibility of both pleasure and new life and that those two things should not be separated. As a result, contraception is either forbidden or not recommended. Because fertility awareness–based contraception does not eliminate the possibility of pregnancy (though it makes it highly improbable), it is an acceptable form of contraception in those traditions. In addition, some women value how this method helps them feel more in tune with their bodies. Probably the biggest benefit, though, is that it does not require any medication or devices, so it is generally inexpensive, has no side effects, and can be reversed at any time.

CONS

Since this method depends on having intercourse only at certain times, it requires abstinence for about one week in four—and at a time when your wife's hormones are most raring to go! As a result, this method can be highly effective when practiced under "perfect use" conditions but doesn't tend to perform as well under "typical use" conditions. And being certain of the fertility window can also be difficult, especially if your wife's periods are irregular (either in general or after pregnancy until they are reestablished). Other ways to monitor fertility, including checking basal temperature and cervical mucus, can be effective, but these require a bit of work, and some women can understandably feel overwhelmed. If this is the method you choose as a couple, do your best to support your wife and take on some of the mental load of keeping track of all these details.

Some couples select this method not because of religious objections to contraception but because they feel it is the most natural. These couples may choose to use barrier methods (condoms) during the fertility week and then enjoy intercourse without barrier methods at "safer" times of the month. Again, this method relies on accurately predicting the fertility window, but if you're careful and can keep track, it can work well.

There is considerable variability in knowledge about fertility awareness–based contraception among healthcare practitioners. If your healthcare provider isn't familiar with ways to track fertility, seek out good books, websites, and support groups that can help.[4]

Barrier Methods (for Him)
HOW IT WORKS

The thin latex barriers called condoms have been the birth control staple for generations. Unrolled onto the erect penis and worn during intercourse, they catch the semen, preventing sperm from entering the uterus and fertilizing the egg. They also protect against most STIs (sexually transmitted infections), so if an STI from a past relationship will continue to be a factor in your marriage, this would be the method of choice.

PROS

Other than in the case of a latex allergy, there are very few side effects. Condoms are readily available without having to see a doctor. They can reduce sensation, which may help men suffering from premature ejaculation or who want to last longer. They also help prevent sexually transmitted infections. Finally, when you decide you want to have a baby, you can easily stop using them.

CONS

Condoms have higher rates of pregnancy than the other methods mentioned, mostly related to imperfect use (with perfect use it is 98 percent effective). They can break your "groove" since you need to stop foreplay to put it on, and you may both have decreased sensation with it on. However, a friend of ours recently had to undergo radiation treatment for cancer and was told by his physician that he would have to use a condom. After not using them for thirty years, he was amazed at how thin they are now!

Barrier Methods (for Her)
HOW IT WORKS

Women can also use barrier devices to stop sperm from entering the uterus. A diaphragm, which looks like half of a ball, can be inserted into the vagina and put in place, covering the opening of the cervix, preventing anything from penetrating. It can be inserted up to six hours before intercourse and should be left in place for at least six hours, and up to twenty-four hours, before removal. Other single-use rings, similar to diaphragms, are also available.

PROS

Diaphragms and rings have few side effects and can be inserted before sex so that it can be more spontaneous. Also, the single-use flexible cups can be used during her period (if the flow isn't too heavy). Some women find this allows for somewhat less messy period sex (although most women find the biggest drawback to sex during her period isn't mess but general discomfort).

CONS

A diaphragm has to be fitted by a physician, which can be invasive. If the diaphragm isn't inserted exactly correctly, sperm can get past it. And checking that it is in properly isn't always easy. As a result, even with perfect use, over the course of a year, about one woman in eight will get pregnant if this is the only method they use. Some women also report difficulty with removing the single-use rings.

Hormonal Methods

When we think of hormonal contraception, we think of "the pill," a name that doesn't make sense since hormonal contraception comes in many different doses of the hormones involved—progestin and estrogen—including some that have only progestin. And pills aren't the only methods of hormonal birth control. Other methods include hormonal injections, skin patches, rods placed under the skin, and vaginally inserted hormonal rings.

HOW IT WORKS

Once each menstrual cycle, a woman's estrogen level peaks, causing ovulation. Hormonal contraception methods remove the estrogen spike and prevent ovulation. They can also increase cervical mucus, which prevents sperm from entering the uterus. Some have expressed concerns that these hormones can have effects on the lining of the uterus, which theoretically could prevent implantation if fertilization occurred. Although no studies have specifically shown this to be a method by which "the pill" works, and the current scientific consensus is that it works by preventing fertilization, this possibility may be an important factor to consider for some.[5]

PROS

Hormonal contraception is a highly effective form of birth control if used correctly. It can also help with other conditions (heavy periods, acne, polycystic ovarian syndrome, PMS) and is often used specifically to treat those conditions.

CONS

The biggest difficulty can be remembering to take it every day (or to change the skin patch or vaginal ring at the proper times). Also, some women experience nausea, bloating, weight gain, "breakthrough" bleeding or mood changes. The manner of stopping the contraception varies based on the type of hormones involved and the method of administration, and it may take a few months for normal cycles to return. This can delay conception when you do decide to have a baby. Some associated health risks (for example, increased risk of breast cancer, stroke, or other cardiovascular problems) also need to be discussed with your healthcare provider as the risks vary based on your individual medical history. There's also the simple cost factor. The average pill costs about $1.50, and it must be taken daily, whether you have sex or not.

Finally, many women claim that the pill affects their libido. The medical literature shows a variable effect,[6] but every time Sheila asks about the pill on her blog, for every woman who says she loves the pill, there's another woman saying something similar to this commenter: "I went on the pill when I was married and never enjoyed sex that much and had trouble climaxing. I had very little sex drive. But when I went off the pill to have children, suddenly my body started responding, and I wanted sex for the first time all on my own! It was like night and day." If your wife is using a hormonal method and her libido has tanked, or she never had much of a libido to begin with, it's worth asking if the contraception method could be contributing to this decline.

Intrauterine Devices
HOW IT WORKS

An intrauterine device (IUD) is a small T-shaped device made of copper or plastic that is placed inside the uterus by a trained health-care provider. IUDs work by thickening cervical mucus, which makes a barrier against the sperm. Also, copper is spermicidal, and the plastic versions release small amounts of hormones that can prevent ovulation. There was concern previously that at least some of the way in which the IUD worked was to prevent implantation after fertilization. This is obviously problematic for people who believe that life begins at conception. But the most recent research seems to indicate that IUDs prevent fertilization, not implantation.[7]

PROS

Of all forms of contraception, IUDs provide one of the lowest pregnancy rates. Once inserted, it requires no further maintenance and can last from three to ten years depending on the model. Once it is removed, fertility rapidly goes back to normal.

CONS

It can change your wife's period. Some women have heavier periods with copper IUDs, and some women stop having periods entirely with some of the plastic IUDs. The biggest drawback is that a trained practitioner needs to place and remove it, and that can be uncomfortable. But it is considered safe and can be done in your healthcare provider's office.

Permanent Birth Control

If you never want to get pregnant again, you can opt for her tubal ligation (having her "tubes tied") or your vasectomy. In a tubal ligation, the fallopian tubes that connect the ovaries to the uterus are ligated (which means cut, then tied off) so that the eggs can't travel to the uterus. In a vasectomy, it is the vas deferens (the tube that sperm use to travel out of the testicles) that is ligated. A vasectomy does not eliminate semen—only the sperm that is in the semen.

Although these procedures can be reversed if someone changes their mind, the chance of fertility returning decreases over time, so think hard before you decide on either of these procedures. Be completely sure you are finished having children, which can be difficult since we can't know the future. You must also be comfortable with the idea of changing your body permanently to prevent having children, which impacts some people more afterward than they thought it would.

One more thing. I (Keith) was floored to hear that Sheila has received emails from many women who "had to have a tubal ligation because their husband refused to have a vasectomy." Wow. Assuming that as a couple you are okay with the idea of permanent contraception, consider the risk of the procedure for each spouse. It is one thing if your wife is already scheduled for a cesarean section for your final child and you decide to do a tubal ligation at the same time, but these women were talking about a different situation entirely! A tubal ligation requires an operating room, anesthesia, and recovery from abdominal surgery. A vasectomy can be done in an office setting under local anesthetic as an outpatient procedure. Whether or not he feels comfortable with permanent contraception, a "good guy" would certainly never feel he has the right to impose it on his wife when it is so much more invasive for her than for him.

So Which One Should You Choose?

Each method has its benefits and drawbacks in terms of effectiveness, cost, ease of use, side effects, and how it affects the sexual experience. Both of you need to consider these factors and decide together in consultation with your healthcare provider. Choose a method that you feel you can stick to consistently, does not have unacceptable side effects for either of you, and is consistent with your beliefs. Different methods may work better at different stages of your life. Many couples use one method before they have children and then switch to another when they're finished having children or during other life changes. Above all, as Christian men—as "good guys"—let's be cautious to follow Paul's instructions to care for our wives as our "own bodies" (Eph. 5:28) when we make these decisions, rather than making them for our benefit at her expense.

CHAPTER 3

Let's Get Frisky!
The Sexual Response Cycle

Now that we know the medical details, let's get to the good stuff about how great sex can feel!

All about the Clitoris

We want to start with the clitoris because great sex for her pretty much always revolves around the clitoris—that small bit of tissue in front of the vagina, between her labia majora. Imagine all the nerve endings in a penis being all squished together on a much smaller surface area. God gave women a part of their bodies with as many nerves as the penis, with no role other than giving her pleasure. The penis has other purposes, but the clitoris has only one.

Okay, timeout for a second. We're going to ask you to do something that might make you feel a bit awkward. Imagine the hand motion that would normally be used when giving a man manual stimulation (or when a guy masturbates), and then imagine the hand motion that would normally be used when giving a woman manual stimulation. Now, *think about which one best resembles intercourse.* Clearly the way the penis is most easily and effectively stimulated mimics intercourse. But the way the clitoris is best stimulated—small movements rubbing back and forth or in circles—doesn't mimic intercourse at all! Plus, all those nerves giving women pleasure aren't located on the vaginal wall, where they would be directly stimulated during intercourse. They're *outside* the vagina. The clitoris tells us that her pleasure is supposed to matter. But since that pleasure isn't usually achieved in the same way your pleasure is, it tells us something *else* about God's design for sex.

God could have made women's bodies so that women would get maximum pleasure from intercourse, but he didn't. That doesn't mean women don't feel pleasure from intercourse or that some don't prefer intercourse to other stimulation. In fact, in the next section of this book, we'll look in detail at how to make intercourse great for her. But in general, most women report that they reach orgasm more easily from direct clitoral stimulation, or at least need a lot of foreplay to reach orgasm through intercourse. Sheila's survey of twenty thousand women found that only 39.4 percent of women who *can* orgasm report being able to do so through intercourse alone. Her survey didn't ask how couples usually reach orgasm, but other research has shown that even if women can reach orgasm through intercourse alone, they do so much more reliably and frequently with direct clitoral stimulation.

This tells us that for a woman to feel pleasure, men have to *slow down and think about their wives*. God made women's bodies so that for each of you to feel pleasure, you'll have to spend some time focusing on her.

Here's something else you need to understand: while sex works best when the man concentrates less on what he's feeling and more on what she's feeling (so as to prolong intercourse and to make her feel good), the opposite is true for a woman. It works best for her if she can stop multitasking in her head, start concentrating on what's happening in her own body, and just let herself experience it. That can be a challenge for many women who tend to have a multitude of thoughts always running through their minds. But for sex to work well, a woman usually has to be a little "selfish" and pay attention to what's going on in her body, and a man has to be unselfish and *also* pay attention to what's going on in her body.

Unfortunately, this reality is not something most guys are prepared for. Most husbands get their knowledge about sex from three sources: the media (including porn), other guys, and their own experience. As a result, we men often have a male-centered view of sex without realizing it. And problems arise when men assume that our way of experiencing pleasure in sex is the right way—as if her experience is not normal. For example, one woman emailed Sheila saying her husband told her, "Sex works fine for me [clearly meaning intercourse alone], and if it doesn't work for you, that's your problem!" Not only is that the exact opposite of what a loving, selfless husband should be like, it is also incredibly unhealthy because it interprets our biologic differences in a way that says I (husband) am working fine and you (wife) are broken—when really we are just biologically different.

Guys, let's commit to seeing our wives as different, not defective. If only 39.4 percent of women who can orgasm can do so through intercourse alone, let's take the approach that says, "If my wife can experience orgasm, I want to do what I can to help her get there!" Let's not be the kind of husband who shrugs and says, "Well, too bad for you then." Foreplay is not the price of admission to the main event; it is a vital part of the sexual experience. Your wife should never feel like the "other stuff" is a burdensome add-on to something that should be quick and easy.

> Guys, let's commit to seeing our wives as different, not defective.

With that as the preamble, let's take a more clinical look at what the male and female sexual response cycles look like.

Sexual Response Cycle

Sex is the building up of pleasurable physical feelings until you reach climax, and then the experience of peace, pleasure, and closeness afterward. The cycle looks like this for some people:[1]

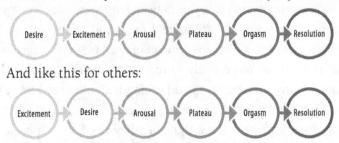

And like this for others:

Notice the difference? Some people experience *spontaneous* desire (often called "libido"), where they want to have sex and even may start to become physically turned on before they start doing anything. Other people feel the desire for sex only after they've started touching one another and getting excited. That's what we'll call *responsive* desire. This difference can be a source of tension if we don't understand it.[2] A few years ago Sheila received a message from this confused man:

> My wife and I have been married almost five years. We've never had a great sex life, but in the last year or so, it's gotten worse. I don't understand why my wife doesn't seem to want me or lust after me the way that I do her. She says she's never been one to feel physically attracted to random guys, but all the other wives in our social circle seem to want their husbands. It's only mine who doesn't. When we do have sex, she enjoys it, but I feel like I always have to talk her into it. I'm a good-looking guy; women are always checking me out. But I just don't turn her on, and I don't get it.

We're going to talk in generalities here, and you may not fit these stereotypes (which is perfectly fine), but generally men tend to be in the first category (spontaneous libido), and women tend to be in the second (responsive libido). Men tend to be more visually stimulated, so sometimes they can see their wife and immediately jump through the desire phase to the excitement phase. (Research is now emerging saying that this may be largely cultural, and many women are very visually stimulated too.[3] And many women can also have spontaneous libidos, though in Sheila's surveys, men were about three times more likely to report this libido dynamic than women.) Many women, on the other hand, aren't turned on in the same way. They don't skip rapidly through desire into excitement simply by a look or a stray thought; they need to be physically warmed up first before desire even registers. And arousal? That doesn't tend to kick in until well after some of that warming up. So there is nothing abnormal or wrong with this man's wife; she sounds like she has a responsive libido, as many women do.

Television shows and movies often portray everyone as having the same sexual response cycle: They see their mate, they start panting, and they make love. So if you're at home and she's not panting, you might figure that she doesn't want you. I have heard many men say something like, "I don't understand it. My wife always says she enjoys sex when we have it, but she never initiates." They wonder, "Does she really enjoy sex, or is she just humoring me? I mean, if she liked it, wouldn't she seek it out?"

But for many women the desire phase simply comes *after* the excitement phase. We found that of women who are reliably aroused by the time sex is finished, 70.9 percent aren't aroused when they start—but they know they'll get there! And women who are always aroused by the end of sex—whether or not they were aroused before all that touching started—reported very positive feelings about sex. So if she's not panting first, that doesn't mean she doesn't want sex or doesn't want you; it just means her libido works differently than yours. For you, desire comes first. For her, it may come after affection and some fooling around. But both of you get to the same place. The solution is not to wait for her to start panting but to give her something to pant about!

> # The solution is not to wait for her to start panting but to give her something to pant about!

Before you jump into action, we have one more word of caution. Not only might your wife need excitement before she feels desire; she might also need different things than you do to feel excited.

When it comes to sexual desire and excitement, women need to be in the right frame of mind before they can move forward. A lot of guys can be pretty heavy-handed when a gentler touch is required. Sheila frequently receives emails from women asking how to get their husbands to stop grabbing their breasts or pinching their butts when they are doing the dishes. Many women consider sexual advances like this intrusive. For these women, the sexual response cycle isn't triggered from a sudden grope but from gentle nonsexual touching.

What if the two of you don't fit these stereotypes? What if your wife is the one with the spontaneous libido, and you're the one with the more responsive libido? This doesn't mean there's anything wrong with you either. Of the twenty thousand women in Sheila's survey, 19.2 percent reported having the higher libido, and many talked about how visually stimulated they were, while many had husbands with a more responsive libido. It's okay for you to need a little longer to warm up too. We have some specific advice for you lower-libido guys about how to help your wife not feel the kind of rejection we have been talking about, but you will have to wait till chapter 10 for that. For now, what we want you to understand is this: *just because you may have different sexual response cycles does not mean one is rejecting the other or doesn't want the other.*

Regardless of the order in which we get there, the excitement phase has characteristic elements that look a little different in men and women. Let's talk about those next.

Excitement
FOR HIM

For guys, the excitement phase is basically a "start your engines" phase when your body gears up for the big event. It is characterized by physical changes that include increased muscle tension, increased heart rate, and more rapid breathing. Blood flow increases to the penis, resulting in an erection. Also, less noticeably, the testicles swell and the scrotum tightens.

The stereotype is that men are always ready for sex, but it is not quite that simple. Men have two routes that result in erections. The first starts in the brain. It may start with something visual or something your wife says or a sexy thought you have and results in a switch being turned on mentally and—there it is! The other path is direct stimulation of the genitals or the areas around the genitals, which can trigger a "reflex erection." The first type is more common in younger years, and the second plays more of a role as we get older.

FOR HER

Since women usually take longer to get warmed up, the excitement phase is all about piquing her desire so her mind and body both want sex. For some women with spontaneous libidos, this stage is very short. For other women, this is the longest of all the stages. If you're married to a woman who takes longer to warm up and you blow right through this step, aiming for the "goal," she's unlikely to find sex pleasurable. Think of this time as being about affection rather than arousal. That means doing everything *but* the really sexy stuff initially. Instead of focusing on erogenous zones, concentrate on other areas, with a lot of kissing, massaging, playing with her hair, or running your fingers along her neck or the insides of her arms. We'll give you more specific tips in part 2 of the book.

As you touch these areas, her body will experience changes. Her breathing will become faster, her nipples will harden, and she'll even get an erection. Yep. That's right. She can get erections too! Blood rushes to the clitoral region, and her clitoris will become engorged and protrude. Plus, she'll get wet. Women's bodies are designed so that when they are aroused, the vagina produces fluid, which makes her genitals slippery so that it's easier for the penis to enter and move around. If she's not wet, the friction won't feel pleasurable. By the end of the excitement phase, you're both ready to move on to more direct sexual stimulation in the arousal phase.

Arousal
FOR HIM

The arousal phase in men is pretty much more of the same. That's probably why men often don't realize that excitement and arousal are two different phases. But there are further changes even after your erection is established: muscle tension heightens, the heart rate and breathing continue to increase, and your erection may become firmer. It is generally not a new type of sensation, though. Women, however, enter a whole new phase.

FOR HER

Once she's aroused, both her body and her mind want sex. That doesn't mean she's ready for intercourse yet—only that her body and mind are now aiming toward it. Now's the time when she'll want more direct stimulation of specific erogenous zones, such as her breasts and her genitals. Her breathing and heart rate will increase, and her areolas (the areas around her nipples) will swell as well.

Plateau
FOR HIM

During the plateau phase, your arousal level stops building and "plateaus," and you stay at that level of arousal until orgasm. For many men, the key is learning to make the plateau phase last longer so that you can give her enough pleasure to get her to orgasm. During this phase (and even earlier in the response cycle) men sometimes release small amounts of semen, called pre-ejaculate, which do contain sperm. Though the quantity isn't large, pregnancy is still possible. That's why we don't recommend the withdrawal method as a form of birth control because you may have already released some sperm before you stop intercourse.

FOR HER

While many sex experts don't differentiate between arousal and plateau, we'd like you to think of these as two distinct phases because the kind of stimulation she'll want during these times is likely different. During excitement and arousal, she'll enjoy being teased, with different techniques, changing things up, changing positions—all helping to build excitement. But once she's reached plateau, she'll want consistency to reach orgasm. The main physical change for her at plateau is that her clitoris will retract under her clitoral hood, becoming flat against the body, getting ready for orgasm.

Orgasm
FOR HIM

When you reach orgasm, your pelvic floor muscles contract about twelve to fourteen times in quick succession, and you'll ejaculate. You won't necessarily feel all those contractions, but you will feel exhilarated. You'll release about five milliliters (a teaspoon) of semen. That may not sound like much, but you'll want to have a towel handy unless you're using a condom. Some men remain at least partially erect for a few minutes after orgasm and can continue intercourse until she reaches orgasm, but that's not terribly common, and such stimulation can feel overly sensitive.

FOR HER

Orgasm feels as good for her as it does for you—but it's not always as obvious! She'll feel that same build up, then a big release. She'll feel her vaginal muscles squeezing involuntarily and rhythmically, her head may thrash around, her legs will go stiff, and her pelvis will automatically tilt upward. She doesn't have a refractory period as you do, so her orgasm can last a long time, with multiple ones on top of each other (though this often takes some work for her to learn how to experience). She can also keep enjoying sex even after she's orgasmed.

As we'll look at later in the book, her easiest routes to orgasm are manual stimulation and oral sex. It often takes some practice to make intercourse orgasmic for her.

Some women also experience "ejaculation" at orgasm, when they expel a large amount of fluid all at once, in a "whoosh." This can be highly pleasurable, but many women also find it embarrassing, worrying that they urinated (don't worry, she didn't). The majority of women do not ejaculate during orgasm, and if she doesn't, there is nothing wrong with her. But if she does, then have fun and roll with it! And keep a towel nearby.

Resolution

After orgasm, all the changes in the body (increased heart rate, erection, muscle tension) slowly return to their resting state, and (for guys) a refractory period follows. Your body releases those hormones (like oxytocin) we talked about earlier. Along with a feeling of closeness to your spouse, most people feel calm and relaxed, to the point of being sleepy.

That's how sex works. We wanted to make sure you know all the physical changes that you both will go through, but you don't have to remember all this, and you don't have to pass a test on it. It is, however, good to have a general idea of how your bodies work so that nothing comes as a surprise and so you know what's normal and what's not.

Now let's turn to the fun part and learn how to make sex the best it can be—in every way.

Part 2

THE THREE COMPONENTS OF GREAT SEX

A Tale of a Mountain and a Snowball

Think of great sex like a luscious, green valley at the bottom of a snow-capped mountain. Over on the other side of the mountain is a desert, with thorny cacti dotting the landscape. Great sex awaits you in the luscious green valley. The cactus-filled desert? Not so much.

Your sex life is like a snowball that starts rolling down that mountain. As it rolls, it grows larger and gains momentum, racing toward the bottom. That momentum represents the habits you develop. They solidify the direction you're going and tend to build on each other, reinforcing what you're already doing.

But what happens if the snowball starts careening down the *wrong* side of the mountain? You have to spring into action to stop it before it gains momentum. You'll have to run ahead of that snowball, halt its descent, and then push it up to the top of the mountain before you can send it back down on the right side. That sounds like a lot of work! Wouldn't it be easier if the snowball started out in the right direction in the first place?

Absolutely! But that may not be as straightforward as it sounds.

Imagine that from the top of the mountain, you can't see the bottom. It's not automatically apparent which route leads to the green valley and which one leads to the desert. All you can see are a bunch of signs. Those signs have arrows, but many are contradictory. You aren't sure which way to go.

That's been the situation for far too many couples. We've been given messages from our wider culture and even from our churches about sex that may sound true but that actually send you tumbling down the wrong side of the mountain. We want to help you recognize which signs to ignore when you're up on top of the mountain and which ones to follow. We're going to do that by delving deeper into what the Bible says about sex and by showing you what our surveys of both men and women have discovered about what makes sex great—and what seriously wrecks it. That way you can avoid the pitfalls and head down the right path from the start. Or if you are already on the wrong path, hopefully we'll help you identify the problem, stop the momentum, and head back up to where things went off track.

If we want to head down the right side of the mountain, we need the right criteria for great sex. That's why we gave you the definition of great sex in the first part of the book. Great sex is sublimely pleasurable, totally mutual, and completely intimate. You should both feel closer after sex, you should both feel physically satisfied after sex, you should both feel as if it is a fun and meaningful part of your marriage. And when you have all that figured out, hopefully that will result in having a lot of sex too!

Before Sheila and I were married, we used to dream about "Saturday sleep-ins," where we'd lie in bed until noon, delighting in each other and having sex as many times as humanly possible until the thought of food grew too enticing. Somehow our schedules and small children never allowed for that, but who doesn't dream of lots and lots of great sex?

These days our Saturday sleep-ins are more likely to take place in an RV. Sheila and I are Canadian, but we spend several months a year in our Minnie Winnie, traveling around North America, and especially the southern US states in the winter, speaking about marriage and sex. Something that always reminds us we've crossed the border is portion sizes. The first time we ordered a large Diet Coke at a northern New York drive-through, we didn't understand what was happening. We were handed a cup so big, it didn't fit in any of our cup holders. It turns out that a Canadian large is an American small.

Bigger is better, we think, whether it's houses, cars, or soft drinks. No matter what it is, the cry is always, What do you want? *More!*

It's natural to want more sex too. In our study, we looked at

How does sex frequency affect marital satisfaction?

More than weekly sex

	Unhappy	Neutral	Happy	Blissful
Men	5.4	28.6	31.4	34.6
Women	10.6	28.5	30.5	30.4

Weekly sex

	Unhappy	Neutral	Happy	Blissful
Men	10.1	38.7	33.5	17.7
Women	16.3	33.9	31.0	18.7

Less than weekly sex

	Unhappy	Neutral	Happy	Blissful
Men	39.5	36.6	18.4	5.5
Women	42.1	30.8	18.4	8.7

0% 10% 20% 30% 40% 50% 60% 70% 80% 90% 100%

■ Unhappy ▨ Neutral ▧ Happy ☐ Blissful

couples with unhappy, neutral, happy, or blissful marriages and noted how frequently they have sex. The trend is undeniable. People who rate their marriages higher tend to have more frequent sex.

But this is a bit of a chicken and an egg thing, isn't it? How do we know which comes first—the relationship or the frequent sex? In our focus groups, we found that when the relationship improved, so did sex. But sex on its own couldn't create a happy relationship. And when sex was happening frequently in a relationship that wasn't happy, it often created more distance.

That's why *more* may not be the right answer when it comes to great sex. We're not saying lots of sex is bad! But couples who rate their sex life only in terms of "how many times a week are we doing it?" are missing the bigger point. If you want those Saturday sleep-ins, here's what we've discovered: frequency is usually the result of a good relationship *outside* the bedroom. Our own research, as well as peer-reviewed literature, leads us to this conclusion: *Healthy, secure people in an emotionally connected marriage who regularly reach orgasm during sex tend to want to have sex.* To put it in terms of an equation, it looks like this:

$$\underset{\text{HEALTH}}{\text{EMOTIONAL}} + \underset{\text{HEALTH}}{\text{PHYSICAL}} + \underset{\text{SECURITY}}{\text{RELATIONAL}} + \underset{\text{CONNECTION}}{\text{EMOTIONAL}} + \underset{\text{SATISFYING SEX}}{\text{PHYSICALLY}} = \underset{\text{SEX}}{\text{WANTING}}$$

Sexual frequency isn't a *thermostat* that we can simply turn up to move us toward great sex. Instead, it's more like a *thermometer* that tells us something about how the relationship is doing. We need the physical, the emotional, and the spiritual connection (or true intimacy) to all be strong if we're going to have great sex. If we follow signs pointing toward those elements of a relationship, we won't end up in the middle of the cactus desert. We'll tell you about each of these elements in turn, but we will start with the one you probably want to get to first anyway—the physical side of sex. Let's jump to creating fireworks!

PHYSICAL
PLEASURE

CHAPTER 4

Mind the Gap!

At any tourist shop in London, England, you'll find T-shirts, mugs, pens—basically anything—with the logo for the London Underground, accompanied by the words *Mind the Gap.* That phrase is famous because at each Underground stop, when the doors open, a pleasant voice warns, "Mind the gap." *Be careful of the gap between the platform and the train.*

Well, guys, it's time for us to mind the gap too.

And we have quite the gap to mind—specifically a 47-point orgasm gap! Sheila's study found that 95.3 percent of men report that they "always or almost always" reach orgasm during sexual encounters.[1] But among women, it's only 48 percent.[2] So to half of you guys reading this: Way to go! You're doing awesome. To the other half: okay, we have some work to do.

On the plus side, we found that most guys are unhappy if their wives aren't reaching orgasm. In fact, they're even unhappier than their wives!

Unfortunately, far too many guys seem to keep on with business as usual—having sex that's not physically satisfying to their wives. One of the biggest shifts we'd like men who read this book to make is to understand that there can't be business as usual if usual means she's not enjoying it. We want fireworks in the bedroom, and that means not only for you but for her too! For sex to be everything

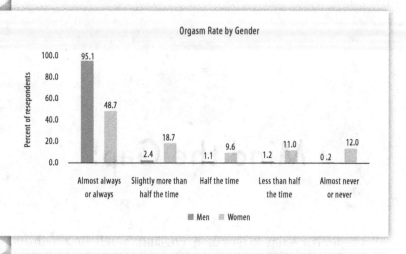

Orgasm Rate by Gender

	Almost always or always	Slightly more than half the time	Half the time	Less than half the time	Almost never or never
Men	95.1	2.4	1.1	1.2	0.2
Women	48.7	18.7	9.6	11.0	12.0

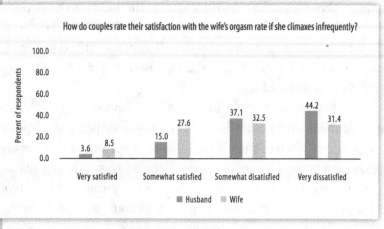

How do couples rate their satisfaction with the wife's orgasm rate if she climaxes infrequently?

	Very satisfied	Somewhat satisfied	Somewhat disatisfied	Very dissatisfied
Husband	3.6	15.0	37.1	44.2
Wife	8.5	27.6	32.5	31.4

it can be, it has to be physically satisfying for both of you. And right now, too many women are missing out.

Let's do a mental exercise to help understand what this orgasm gap feels like from a woman's perspective. Imagine a world where what women need to feel loved is to go out to eat at a restaurant at least once a week, where you talk and enjoy a delicious meal. This is the pinnacle of marriage to her.

Picture a couple, Tracey and Doug, who tries to live by this. One

Tuesday night our intrepid couple heads to a restaurant. They order appetizers, a main course, and a dessert.

The waitress arrives with Tracey's appetizer—a steaming bowl of cheese and broccoli soup. Tracey finishes it and declares it delicious. But nothing comes for Doug. Then Tracey's steak arrives. Doug's still wondering where his appetizer is, but Tracey starts slathering the butter and sour cream onto the baked potato and takes a bite of the steak with peppercorn sauce and asparagus. She declares it scrumptious.

Now Tracey is finished with her steak, and the waitress heads toward the couple again. In front of Tracey she places a steaming, luscious molten lava cake. Tracey squeals in delight as she scoops some out. Just as she's down to the last few spoonfuls, the waitress finally arrives with Doug's chicken wing appetizer. Doug's ecstatic, and he digs in, eating one quickly, and then another. But before he can get to his third one, Tracey stands up, ready to go home. "Dinner was amazing," she declares as she heads for the door. He follows behind her, glancing at the uneaten chicken wings still on his plate, while Tracey says, "I love doing this with you!"

Imagine that Doug and Tracey faithfully do this every week for ten years. How do you think Doug will feel about eating at restaurants?

The sad reality is that for too many women, that is exactly what sex is like, *year after year after year*. What would happen if instead of accepting a woman's lack of orgasm as normal, we considered it a vital part of sex? What would happen if, when we got married, we focused first and foremost on helping her feel comfortable, experience arousal, and reach orgasm, rather than simply having intercourse with her?

When it comes to couples' satisfaction with sex in marriage, the orgasm gap tells the majority of the story. If you think of her orgasm as secondary, then when she takes a longer time to reach orgasm than you do, she will feel self-conscious, like she's imposing. When she needs something beyond what you need to orgasm, she will feel something is wrong with her, like she is broken. If your orgasm is the standard, then when it isn't happening for her, she will tend to internalize the problem and blame herself for it. And the worst part is that this will make orgasm *even more difficult* for her. If, instead, you both believed that sex wasn't really sex unless you both enjoyed it, then her lack of enjoyment wouldn't be *her* problem, it would be *your* challenge to work through together.

When Women's Pleasure Isn't Prioritized, Sex Eventually Dries Up

Sheila once wrote a blog post about how many men feel that foreplay is optional, and in reply a commenter said,

> Indeed. I'm married to such a guy. I'm really puzzled. Where on earth does this idea come from? I know it is not out of malice. He really is convinced foreplay does not "belong." It is not that he would not want me to have any pleasure. He rather takes for granted that I automatically do.

Another woman told this story:

> Immediately after my husband and I were married, I started having frequent and painful UTIs. After every sexual encounter, no matter how many prevention techniques I used, I always had an infection and was constantly running to the doctor and on antibiotics. After six months of this, I was ready to never have sex again. Instead of receiving compassion from my husband, he said we needed to have more sex. His logic was that my body needed to adjust to being a wife, and the quicker that happened the better. And so the mindset was reinforced that sex is not for me. My pleasure has nothing to do with it. This is an extremely hard mindset

to break. The UTIs finally started to lessen when another medical issue was cleared up. But I have never recovered from this horrible start. After all these years, sex is a duty, and I can count on two hands the orgasms I have had. I want an intimate and passionate sex life, and I need compassion and selflessness from him in the bedroom. I hope all husbands understand that.

In a marriage where her pleasure is neglected, what happens to their sex life in the long run? In our men's survey, we found in every metric we used that guys who report they don't spend enough time on foreplay are consistently less happy with their sex lives. They also report that their wives are less happy with their sex lives *and* they're less happy in their marriages in general. Lack of orgasm in women is a "canary in the coal mine." It's saying there is something—or a lot of things—off track. And those problems affect the happiness of *both* spouses.

How does infrequent female orgasm affect a couple's sexual satisfaction? (How many times more or less likely are they to experience the following?)	
I spend enough time on foreplay that my wife is aroused when we begin having sex	-6.6
I am satisfied with the amount of closeness I share with my wife during sex	-3.3
I am satisfied with the amount of enthusiasm my wife shows in the bedroom	-2.7
My wife is able to communicate her sexual desires and preferences with me	-2.7
I am satisfied with the amount of adventure my wife shows in the bedroom	-2.5
I am able to communicate my sexual desires and preferences with my wife	-1.7
My wife makes my sexual pleasure a priority when we have sex	-1.4

Women have the capacity to derive great pleasure from sex. They may take longer to warm up, but when they reach orgasm, they can have multiple orgasms! They don't have a refractory period as men do, so they can have prolonged, intense enjoyment if things are done right. A husband can unlock incredible sexual responsiveness in his wife if, rather than seeking only his own pleasure, he does everything he can to ensure that she also enjoys it. And here's how to do it.

Put Your Pleasure On Hold Till You Figure It Out for Her

If you've been "going out to dinner" for years where you get to feast while an empty plate is placed before her, then for the next little while, give up food yourself until you make sure that she is fed as well. Or, if you are just starting out in marriage, make a commitment from the beginning to ensure she gets fed as much as you do!

Here's why: every time you have sex, or ask for sexual favors like oral sex or manual stimulation, and she does not reach orgasm, you solidify in her mind that sexual pleasure is for you and not for her. *Every. Time.* You will always orgasm more than your wife because her orgasm is far more dependent on her mood, hormone levels, stress, and so on. The orgasm gap is unlikely ever to completely close. But consistently having sex when your wife is not enjoying it cements in her mind that sex is something she does for you, not for her.

When you ask her to give you "favors" when she has yet to reach orgasm in any way, or when orgasm happens very rarely for her or when it is the last thing on her mind at that time, she is likely to find these requests off-putting and distinctly *un*sexual. She might even develop an aversion to anything sexual because to her it feels shallow, like a rejection. If God made sex to be a deep knowing, then that means *both* people need to matter. But if in your relationship sex is primarily about your physical needs, then it communicates to her that she is irrelevant. That can kill her ability to reach orgasm.

Consider Her Orgasm a Main Aim of Sex

We should assume that her frequent orgasm is our aim during sex—not necessarily every time, but it should be the norm. Unfortunately, we found that the vast majority of men felt they were prioritizing their wife's pleasure and felt they were doing enough foreplay, even when their wife wasn't orgasming the majority of the time. For instance, 99.3 percent of men whose wives frequently orgasm believe they make their wife's pleasure a priority. But so do

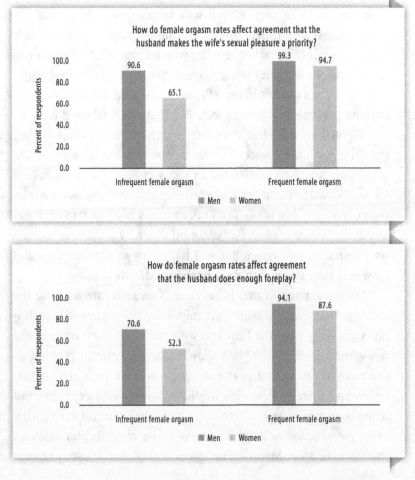

90.6 percent of men whose wives don't orgasm frequently! We have to ask: Why are we guys giving ourselves such good marks?

Help Her Think Differently about Sex

Most husbands *are* eager and willing to put their wives' pleasure first, but sometimes the women are the ones uncomfortable with that.[3] Telling her you want to work on figuring out the orgasm piece for her may even cause her to panic. She may still want to focus on you because doing so serves other purposes in her mind: it may make her feel like she's a good wife because she's been told you need these things to feel loved. Aiming for your physical release may make her feel safe because she worries that without it you will watch porn or lust after other women. Some women even struggle with the idea of having an orgasm and seem more comfortable going without because to enjoy sex feels like they're somehow dirty.

Women in evangelical circles are frequently told that they should enjoy having sex even if they don't orgasm, because of how important sex is to husbands.[4] In focus groups Sheila conducted for her book *The Great Sex Rescue*, she talked to many women who didn't reach orgasm but who still desired sex because it made them feel close to their husbands. We found that 62.7 percent of women who infrequently orgasm are still happy about the intimacy and closeness they share with their husbands during sex.

But how much of this is because of women internalizing the message that their pleasure isn't important? To return to our dinner saga, imagine if the husband were told, "Don't be upset about not getting your dinner; you should take pleasure in how much she enjoyed eating and in the closeness you felt from the conversation you shared." Few men would be willing to accept this. But when it comes to sex, Christian women have been hearing that exact message for so long! It's one of those misdirection signs on that mountaintop. Many women won't fight for their own orgasms because they grow up hearing that sex is a man's need, not a woman's, and giving him release is her duty.[5] As a result, you may be dedicated to helping her reach orgasm, but she may not share the same aim. After all, 36.1 percent of women who don't reliably reach orgasm report not being bothered by it.

Even so, guys, that is not a license to keep "using" her. She may say, "Go ahead, don't worry about me," but you know her pleasure should matter. So be the hero she needs! By consistently telling her that her pleasure is important, you can help your wife reconnect with her sexuality. No matter what her roadblocks are, even if they aren't of your making, you are the one whom God has given the job of helping her unlock her sexuality. It's part of loving her as you love your own body.

We're not saying that she has to orgasm every time, but she should *most* of the time. You both should be giving during sex, not just her. Now, giving doesn't always need to mean orgasm; it may mean a prolonged massage or talking and kissing for a long time. But both should be routinely giving of themselves for the other person and regularly ensuring that the other person receives something wonderful and satisfying from sex.

Most of all, even if you've had trouble for years and she has yet to reach orgasm at all, remember this: *she is not broken.* Her clitoris is not broken. Her vagina is not broken. She may simply have roadblocks that you can help her dismantle. Maybe she feels shame from past messages about sex and needs to work through these with a licensed counselor or to read *The Great Sex Rescue.* Maybe she has sexual abuse in her past and needs to seek out a licensed therapist specializing in trauma. Maybe she has sexual pain and needs to see a pelvic floor physiotherapist. Maybe she has betrayal trauma from your past porn use, and you need to give her time without pressure to trust you again. Wherever she's at, remember that *her body* is not the problem. The more that you see her body as the problem, the worse the problem becomes. Instead, work to identify the issue, and then be her hero and help her fix it.

CHAPTER 5

Going Back to Square One

We know you want to rock your wife's world and you're on board with helping her orgasm, so you're likely anticipating some specific instructions right about now: how to rub her clitoris, how to touch her breasts, how to perform oral sex well. You might be hoping we'll teach you all about technique that will rock her world.

But we're not going to do that.

And it's not because we're squeamish. Seriously, you would not believe the questions we answer in anonymous Q&As at our marriage events! We can say terms like *clitoris* and *ejaculation* and *oral sex* without batting an eye. But we're not going to give step-by-step instructions because the problem is usually not that couples are *using the wrong techniques* as much as that they are *skipping important steps*. Once you figure out those steps, the technique piece often takes care of itself.

So let's go back to those first principles.

Learning the Steps to Arousal

Why is it that parents worry so much about teenagers making out? Are we paranoid about kissing itself? Nope, not usually. Instead, it's that we know that when you kiss passionately, after a while your body will start to want more. Certain areas of your anatomy might feel like they're on fire. They will want to be touched. So hands will naturally start exploring. That will make the fire even bigger. And the long, drawn-out make-out session gets our teenage lovebirds so aroused that they do things they weren't planning on.

Arousal, you see, follows a natural progression. Our bodies have certain arousal steps, and each step readily leads to the next:

- Low-key physical contact that makes you feel close
- Kissing and low-key touching that is drawn out and makes you feel breathless and start to feel aroused
- Touching erogenous zones while kissing and learning what feels good
- Removing some clothing and learning to touch each other without awkwardness

From there our bodies tend to get hot and bothered and want to head toward orgasm, either through intercourse or another route.

Our bodies are meant to respond in a certain order. Great sex is a progression from one step to the next. Orgasm for a woman is mostly about learning the skill of listening to her body, knowing when she wants to go to the next step, and then riding the wave of pleasure to take her even further along that progression. She has to be able to let that pleasure carry her along, like a surfer riding a wave. And it's the "listening to your body" piece that has mysteriously been turned off for many women. If you jump to the next step before her body cries out for it, or if you skip steps, then there's no way she can learn to listen to her body because it isn't saying anything yet.

Why is it that dating couples find it difficult to stop themselves from going further during a make-out session? Maybe because the couple isn't planning on having intercourse—or trying for orgasm!

All they intend to do is kiss, and so they hang out there for a while. It becomes more and more passionate, and they find they enjoy it. And because they spend time enjoying it, their bodies respond and practically cry out to do more!

Once you're married, though, you're suddenly allowed to go all the way to intercourse. And that's what often happens. Too often couples go straight from light kissing to intercourse with little in between. The results are predictable. She doesn't feel much of anything, so she ends up assuming she doesn't like sex, he ends up agreeing and wondering if she's broken, and her arousal stops.

The couple may then seek out information on how to make sex feel good for her. They learn all about "clitoral stimulation"—stimulating the clitoris through oral or manual means—and they may learn about how most women like their breasts touched, and so they try that. But again, that repeats the same problems! They're going straight to heavy petting without all the other action beforehand.

Let's revisit that sexual response cycle we talked about earlier. If you remember, for most women, it looks like this:

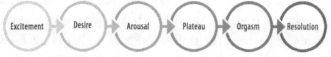

Think about the excitement phase as the flirty and affectionate things a couple does early in the sexual progression—like kissing and nibbling on someone's ear. For most women, the desire for sex doesn't kick in until those first steps awaken it. Then the arousal phase includes touching that's more intentional. You're not only being affectionate, you're trying to arouse each other. How do you know what stage she is at? Well, once she's feeling excited and she does want sex (desire has kicked in), then certain parts of her body will want to be touched. *Her body will start speaking to her.* That's what you're aiming for. Many women, unfortunately, have a hard time listening to their bodies. We'll go over how you can help in a minute. But the first thing you need to understand is that gradually increasing states of arousal is how the vast majority of women reach orgasm. This is the typical female sexual response.

It's no surprise that many men don't understand this progression. It goes against what you see in the movies. It also likely goes against your experience as a man. For you, sex may work just fine if you jump in at any point. You may even be tempted to see kissing and prolonged touching as what you settle for before you're married, but after marriage you see them as unnecessary because now you can get to the good stuff. But that is not, generally, how women work. Unless she experiences sex as a progression, she's unlikely to get to the good stuff. She can't learn to reach orgasm unless she figures out when her body is telling her to move to the next phase. And she can't do that unless sex is a natural sequence where one thing leads to the next *because her body wants it.* If desire hasn't kicked in because excitement hasn't happened, you can rub, bop, and twist to your heart's content, and her body won't say a thing to her.

> Great sex isn't found by following a blueprint. Sexuality is awakened when it's *personal* and *passionate.*

Unfortunately, sex advice often replaces this idea of progression with a blueprint you're supposed to follow. But great sex isn't found by following a blueprint. Sexuality is awakened when it's *personal* and *passionate.* Think about a Shakespearean love sonnet. What makes it powerful is the emotions behind the words, not the number of syllables in each line or which word rhymes with which. Reducing sex to a series of boxes like some preflight checklist is the opposite of great sex. "Remove clothing. *Check.* Clitoral stimulation commencing. *Check*." That's not sexy. And that's why step-by-step instructions on how to get her aroused don't work. If, instead of moving through steps at her pace, you obediently follow some protocol, she'll feel like a science experiment or a zoo exhibit. One newlywed woman explained it like this:

> I'm just starting to figure out my body, and I know that I can reach orgasm now through touching myself. I want my husband to be able to help me as well, but we'll have sex, and then he'll be down between my legs, rubbing randomly, looking at my face to see if it's having any effect, with this expression going between me being a science experiment and him being a sad puppy. Half the time I just push him away and tell him, it's okay, we can just go to sleep.

Sad puppies are not sexy. Impersonal scientists are not sexy. Looking at your watch to see how long she's taking is not sexy. These reactions take her out of the moment and make her worry about what you're feeling. Instead, you want her to think about her own body and what it is saying to her so that you can help her work through the arousal steps at her own pace.

Why Do Many Women Have a Hard Time Listening to Their Bodies?

Okay, so now you have a plan! Start at the beginning of the sexual response cycle and gradually go forward from there, and things will work much better.

Theoretically, yes. Unfortunately, real life doesn't always work that way. Why? Well, many women have spent their entire teenage and young adult years training themselves *not* to become aroused. Girls are told many statements growing up that reinforce this: "Boys will push sexual boundaries. You need to stay alert and make sure they don't go too far." "Boys can pass a point of no return and be unable to stop. You need to be the gatekeeper." It is the girl's job not only to control her own urges but also to make sure they as a couple don't go too far.[1] He's the accelerator, she's the brakes.

Picture a make-out session with your wife before you were married (even if you had sex before marriage). Chances are you were enjoying it, your body was responding, and it was feeling great. The same may have been true for her too. But what was going on in her head may have been quite different from what was in yours. "Should I stop him now? Is his breathing getting too heavy? Where's his hand going? Am I still in control?" The last one is critical. "Am I still in control?" Many women have trained themselves to stay in control so well that even when they're allowed to get hot and heavy, they find it hard to let go. Staying vigilant has become a reflex.[2]

A woman in one of Sheila's focus groups described it like this: "I felt like I was outside my body, judging what was going on. I was always on the alert, and so I never really experienced what was happening. I was instead watching, judging, being on guard. And I could never figure out how to turn that off once I married."

Many women are like that: frustrated, desperately wanting to discover the magic key to unlock orgasm but having such a hard time relaxing and just experiencing. Your job is to help your wife relax and learn to overcome those barriers by helping her learn to listen to her body.

You may feel like you are already trying to do that and wonder why it doesn't seem to be working. Well, it might be that you are only one voice fighting against many others from church, books, websites, movies, and even youth group events back in high school that primed her brain into thinking, "Sex is not safe, it is not for you, and you're a bad person if you enjoy or want it." But don't despair; all hope is not lost! You may be just one voice, but you are the most important one. You can be the one consistent voice that says, "This is for you." Even if you've made mistakes in the past that you need to apologize to your wife for, even if you've accidentally cemented some negative beliefs about sex in your wife's brain, *you have a chance to help her redeem and rediscover her sexuality.* Your voice can constantly affirm her: "This is meant to feel amazing for both of us!"

> *You have a chance to help her redeem and rediscover her sexuality.*

Reassure her that you truly enjoy making her feel good. Consistently show with your actions that you want sex to be mutually satisfying. If she keeps saying, "Don't worry about me," don't leave it at that. Maybe she needs to be challenged: "Well, my love, I want this to be something that is amazing for both of us. So when *do* we worry about you?"

As you make her the center of attention and focus on unlocking her sexuality, remember to start with the natural progression and work with her body. Concentrate first on helping her feel aroused, rather than expecting her to reach orgasm right away. Enjoy the journey rather than trying to find the most direct route to intercourse.

What If You've Been Married for a While and Her Orgasm Is Still Elusive?

Sheila here! In our research on women's marital and sexual satisfaction, we conducted interviews and focus groups with women who had struggled with orgasm but now really enjoy sex. And you know what they told us? They didn't list techniques they tried or grumble about how horrible sex was before. No, they spent the majority of the interviews gushing over how loving, patient, and Christlike their husbands had been while they were figuring out the orgasm piece. Many of these women had gone years without orgasming, and their husbands never knew. The women had faked it, assured the husbands they were excellent lovers, and pretended to enjoy sex—all while feeling disappointed. But when their husbands realized that their wives were not feeling pleasure during sex, they stepped up to the plate big time. And every single one of those women who volunteered for that focus group credits her learning to orgasm to her husband's patience and humility as they went back to square one.

We also talked to many women whose husbands *did* know they weren't orgasming, but it took years for the couple to decide this wasn't acceptable anymore. Sometimes she had been repeatedly bringing up the issue, and he would become angry or hurt and brush her off. But even in those marriages, when he decided to make her sexual enjoyment as much of a priority as his own, when he realized she was made to orgasm too and that he *could* figure it out, those marriages were totally turned around. It took some men longer, but eventually they all learned the secret to mutually orgasmic sex.

No matter where you are in your marriage—whether you've known this is a problem since day one or if you've been blindsided—you can do this! You can learn to study your wife, to love every inch of her, to truly "know" her inside and out. You can embrace true mutuality in sex as a way to cherish, love, and honor the woman you have pledged your life to. Now let's look at how to unlock her sexuality!

CHAPTER 6

Ladies First
(All about Orgasm)

"Ladies first" isn't only for when you're going through doorways, scrambling off sinking ships, or getting first crack at the turkey on Thanksgiving. It's also for orgasm.

And that's the way God made women's bodies! Once women understand their bodies and can "ride the wave" to orgasm, many can keep that orgasm going for quite a while and even have multiple orgasms. You can thrust to your heart's content (or to the content of other body parts), and she can keep climaxing the whole time! *Sex works best when she goes first.*

There's also the simple practical element. No matter how generous a guy you are, no matter how much you *intend* to bring her to orgasm, if she doesn't reach orgasm before you do, hormones can overrule the best of intentions. At climax, all those hormones coursing through your body tell you very, very loudly, *You want to go to sleep now.* If you try to rock her world while everything inside is telling you, *Relax, it's time to stop*, it will likely end in disappointment. She'll know you're tired, which means she'll feel pressure to hurry up. And adding pressure is the quickest way to quash any chance of her reaching orgasm. Here's how one woman described her situation:

I'm worried that I have subconsciously taught myself not to experience any pleasure during intercourse because I usually don't get even mildly aroused until my husband is almost done. I've thought about this a fair bit, and I think it's because I know that stopping at a bit of arousal every time, and not getting to orgasm, leaves me feeling so unsatisfied. I suppose I've convinced myself that it's more satisfying to watch him have fun than it is to start having fun myself, but then not finish. Yes, we have tried to focus on me after he's climaxed, but then I always feel bad because he's obviously spent, and then my "feeling bad" stops it from happening anyways . . . so subconsciously I go back to square one: "Why bother allowing myself to get turned on in the first place?"

She assumes that if she gets any pleasure, it will be only after he has climaxed. But by the time that happens, she feels guilty about making him do the work. She later elaborated:

I suppose it's time to explain all this to him somehow. I worry, though, that my husband, who is under a ton of stress already, will end up feeling a huge load of guilt. He knows it's extremely tough for me to orgasm (honestly, I'm not sure if I've actually had a real, full orgasm in our almost ten years . . . maybe? I've never been absolutely sure). And I've done an unfortunately good job of convincing him that I'm content enough because I just figure I'm one of the defective ones and that I should be happy with what I do have . . . a wonderful, godly husband who knows he's very, very loved and who is sexually satisfied.

Well, we would suggest that a good, godly husband would not want his wife to be able to write that email! A good, godly husband would prioritize her orgasm, would not assume that she's broken, and would not be satisfied with simply making himself happy. So let's figure out how you good, godly husbands can get there!

Recognize Her Best Route to Orgasm

Maybe you're a newlywed still trying to figure out sex, or even an engaged guy who's excited to start his sex life with his new wife! That's awesome because you're starting from scratch. Your wife may be someone who orgasms fairly easily, or she may take some time to learn to relax and let herself feel pleasure. Either way, for most women it's far easier to orgasm through manual or oral stimulation than through intercourse. Remember from chapter 3 that in our survey, only 39.4 percent of women who can orgasm report being able to with intercourse alone.

Your first job, then, is to help her reach orgasm in whatever way is easiest for her. Intercourse may not be what brings your wife ecstasy. Don't just get her aroused and then start intercourse assuming it is all a matter of timing. Most women don't orgasm if you only have intercourse—even women who orgasm during every sexual encounter. Among women who reliably orgasm, 55.3 percent can't do so without direct clitoral stimulation. Yes, it's wonderful if both of you reach orgasm during intercourse—and we'll talk about how to make that more likely in a minute—but you're not a failure if it never happens. Sex involves everything sexual you do together, not just intercourse. If what brings her the most pleasure is

> Sex involves everything sexual you do together, not just intercourse.

something else, then that can be a focus of your sex life together too. Your job is to figure out what that *something else* is.

If you've been married for a while and orgasm has rarely or never happened for her, you could be sending that snowball down the wrong side of the mountain, toward the cactus desert. If you truly want great sex, then it's time to chase after that snowball, push it back up the mountain, and start again at the beginning. Tell her you want to make sex about both of you, and that means focusing on figuring out her orgasm first. Help undo the mindset (which you may have reinforced) that sex is not for her. Help her learn to listen to her body. Start with finding out what gets her aroused. And apologize for not doing so earlier.

Practice the Art of Never Being in a Hurry

Do you know why women take so long to reach orgasm? Because men can reach it so quickly! The only reason we think women take a long time to reach orgasm is because *compared to men* they do. On average, women take about fourteen minutes to reach orgasm from the time they are aroused (and up to twenty minutes or so is not atypical).[1] The average man takes about five minutes.[2] But what if the average man took forty-five minutes? Then she'd look like a rocket!

The problem is not the amount of time she takes. The problem is that *compared to you* she'll tend to take longer. Combine that with the messages she's received—that foreplay is extra and not necessary; that sex is intercourse; that husbands need to orgasm or they'll be depressed, sad, and impossible to live with—and you can see how she may struggle to relax long enough to experience the pleasure she needs to feel. Unfortunately, you can add to her struggle by how you act during sex, and we know that's the last thing you want to do! So no sighing and staring at your watch. No asking, "Why isn't this working yet?" And certainly no "sad puppy dog eyes" that she's taking too long. Your mission, should you choose to accept it (and you should!), is to make her feel like you have all the time in the world.

Now, what do you do with that time?

Learn How She Likes to Be Touched

Communicate in the Moment

You can't make her feel good if you don't know how she's feeling. But your wife may not always be comfortable speaking up about what feels good, especially if she is self-conscious. Or she may not know how to describe what she's feeling. Or you may not understand what she is getting at. What does she mean by *faster, harder,* or *more*? What does she mean by *not there, up a bit more*? If you don't understand what she means and you don't say anything, she may start worrying whether you feel awkward or like you're failing. And since there's no way she can listen to her body when her focus is on your feelings, you have to master this. Here's how:

Practice on a Nonerogenous Zone

Practice giving and receiving instructions that have nothing to do with sex. Tell her to describe the following:

a. a particular nonerogenous spot on her body that she wants touched (say, two inches down on her left shoulder blade) and

b. exactly how she wants it touched (rubbed slowly in circles, rubbed fast, what level of pressure, and so on).

Because this practice has nothing to do with sex, there's no pressure or reason for her to feel self-conscious or worried about you. She can explain what she wants you to do, and you can learn what she means by *faster, harder, softer,* or *push lightly* without any stress. Once you've done one movement, practice another on a different body part.

Warming Up: The Excitement Phase

Since physical response is about both mental desire and physical desire, you can't jump right to the "good stuff" first! You have to build up to it. When you start to get frisky, imagine her erogenous zones as having big "No Trespassing" signs. You need special permission to move beyond those signs. Until then, you're warming up her senses and helping her to relax, to get out of her head, and to focus on what's going on.

For women, orgasmic sex often starts by gentle, tender, loving actions that help her mentally step out of "mom/work/stress" mode and relax into "feeling like a woman" mode. Start with cuddling and maybe running your fingers along each other's arms, necks, shoulders, backs, legs, and so on. Use innocent physical touch that's relaxing but can get some goosebumps going. Work *with* her body and her mental state rather than imposing something upon it. If she's stressed out by everything on her to-do list, going straight to whispering what you want to do to her tonight may cause her to shut down. But starting with a back rub while you talk about your days, then snuggling while you both trace your fingers over each other, then kissing, then moving to some under-the-clothes touching, and then—*after* her heart is racing a little—saying those racy remarks is a lot more likely to bring on the fireworks you're looking for.

> Imagine her erogenous zones as having big "No Trespassing" signs.

> Work *with* her body and her mental state rather than imposing something upon it.

- Stroking her hair
- Stroking the insides of her arms and behind her knees
- Nibbling at her ear
- Kissing her neck
- Rubbing her neck
- Rubbing her feet

Reaching the Arousal Phase

If she starts to relax and moan, then she's moved from the excitement phase to the arousal phase, with desire kicking in! Now you can move on to more erogenous areas—her breasts, between her thighs, her genitals. What most women find erotic and pleasurable is the build-up. Start kissing at her feet and move up the insides of her legs toward her genitals, or start at the belly button and move up to her breasts or down toward her clitoris. Don't jump right to those areas. Take your time, circle for a bit, and then go in, but *slowly.*

The clitoris is awfully small, but it's awfully important. You need to figure out where it is, and you need to get comfortable finding it. Have her show you. Look at it. Play around a bit so you know what it feels like!

How do you rub it in a way that feels pleasurable? Think of her vulva like a clock, with 12:00 being right above her clitoris, and 6:00 being the bottom opening of her vagina, pointing toward the anus. The clitoris usually enjoys being touched from the direction of 12:00, not from the direction of 6:00 (like, go down, don't go up). Between the clitoris and the vagina is the urethra, the opening where urine is expelled, and that feels distinctly unsexy if it's stimulated. If you rub there, you can kill the mood. When she's just starting the arousal stage, often circles or figure eights or even going back and forth feels good. Later on, she may simply need the clitoris pressed down against her body. The key is communication.

- Direct stimulation of her clitoris with your fingers or your tongue
- Inserting your fingers in her vagina, especially stimulating the top of her vaginal wall (the side that's toward her belly button, where the "G-spot" region is). Think of it as making a "come here" motion with your finger.
- Fondling her breasts by rubbing your hands lightly over them, squeezing them a bit, or lightly touching her nipples
- Licking or sucking her nipples

And don't forget to keep kissing! One study of over fifty thousand adults found that women were more likely to have reached orgasm in their last sexual encounter if that encounter included deep kissing, even more likely than if it included intercourse. Expressing love during sex is key to women's sexual response.[3]

Other than that, we're not going to tell you specifically what to do in these areas. We don't want to be the directors of your sex life. The key is not what *we* think you should do but what *your wife* wants you to do and what feels good for *her*. Some of the ideas we listed may be total turn-offs for your wife even at the height of her arousal, and she may be wild about ideas that aren't on our list. Learning how to communicate with each other about what you're both feeling and helping her learn to relax and "ride the wave" are what will bring the fireworks! So use those skills you fostered in the exercise about communication to learn whether she likes you to focus on her vagina, her clitoris, or both, and in what order; whether she likes her breasts being fondled or sucked or neither; whether she prefers oral or manual stimulation. This isn't paint-by-numbers, it is learning about your own wife. And realize that it might change from encounter to encounter. Don't assume what worked last time is what she wants tonight. Stay sensitive to the signs she gives you each time.

And ask questions! One "game" that Sheila has been recommending on her blog for years is to play "optometrist." And, no, this has nothing to do with eyesight, although if looking turns you on, all the better. When you go for an eye test, they have you look through a bulky machine while they give you options: "Which is better? A or B?" And once you answer "B," then they compare B and C. You can do the same with sex! Does she like her clitoris stroked like this or like that? What about her nipples? Which is better? A or B? She may find it easier to answer that question than to answer, "What do you want me to do now?" or "How should I touch you?" Give her some options and pay attention. But make sure it is light and fun, not a science experiment.

> Expressing love during sex is key to women's sexual response.

Building toward Orgasm: The Plateau Phase

Varying what you're doing and even stopping and starting can build arousal during early stages. But once she is fully aroused, consistency is key. Vary things at this stage and she'll get frustrated.

As you enter the plateau phase, building to orgasm, remember that what got her going earlier may not be what she desires now. She doesn't want teasing as much as she wants things more direct. Earlier she may not have liked her nipples or breasts being touched; now she may like her nipples touched hard or even pinched. Start out soft, teasing, and playful, but once she's feeling good and heading for orgasm, steady, consistent, and firm are what she's looking for!

What about Touching You?

You'll notice that in these suggestions of how to figure out what feels good, we've left out anything about how she should touch you. That's because to become aroused and reach orgasm, most women need to concentrate on what they are feeling. If she starts touching you and trying to bring you pleasure, that can cause her to lose focus and make arousal more difficult for her.

That doesn't mean she'll never touch you. Once you've figured out how her body works and you both have confidence in her ability to reach orgasm, then she will enjoy trying to stimulate you as well. And before that, since part of becoming orgasmic for some women is becoming more comfortable with sexuality in general, she may need to explore both her body and yours without pressure to orgasm or make anyone feel good. She may discover that she is indeed a sexual being when she sees the dramatic effect she can have on you. But when you're first learning how to bring her to orgasm, it needs to be part of her journey of discovery, not done with the end goal of having your needs met.

Give Her Permission to Say "Stop"

Feeling self-conscious about receiving pleasure can be one of the biggest roadblocks to orgasm for women. If you sense that she's zoned out and excitement isn't building, stop what you're doing and reconnect emotionally. Remind her that sex is for both of you and that you want to do the work to study her and learn how best to love her. Show her that she can speak up if she wants you to do something differently (or even to stop entirely) if it's not feeling good, without worrying you'll feel angry or cheated. The large study we mentioned earlier also found that a key to a woman's reaching orgasm is being able to express when something doesn't feel good.[4] Knowing you care enough to change gears when necessary will make her feel safe.

How to Reach Orgasm during Intercourse

Once you're able to bring her to orgasm reliably (let's say at least half the time) with oral or manual stimulation, you'll likely want to try to help her reach orgasm through intercourse.

Let her be the one to tell you when to enter her, either by taking your penis with her hand, opening her legs more, or pulling you on top of her. Allow her to invite you in, rather than barging ahead when she may not be ready. Even if she's well-lubricated, before you move ahead, she needs to decide mentally, "Let's do this!"

Some women, though, may be saying, "Let's do this!" without being lubricated. Women's lubrication levels often vary throughout the month, with their hormone cycles, and can drastically fall after menopause. That can make a husband wonder if she's actually excited. One man told us the following story:

> I used to think my wife was faking. She'd act all excited and would tell me she wanted me to start intercourse, but she'd barely be wet. But we've realized that over the course of the month, her lubrication really changes. She's often really into it mentally, but she just doesn't get that lubricated. She still reaches orgasm, though! I've learned to trust what she says more than her lubrication level, and she's promised me she won't ever pretend she's into it when she's not.

Water-based lubricants are safe, easy to use, and available at drugstores. They can make sex a much more pleasurable experience and alleviate a lot of worry over whether she'll be lubricated enough.

The key to bringing her to orgasm during intercourse is knowing when to transition from other sexual play. Start too early and she may not be aroused enough to go over the edge before you do. Remember that she gets a lot more direct stimulation from you rubbing her than she does from intercourse. So her arousal level might be building and building, but when you transition it can drop off, and you might need to play catch-up. It's important to figure out what works for her. Does she like you to tease her a bit once you start, going shallow and then going deeper only once she asks? Or would she prefer that you wait until she's very aroused, and then go deep all at once? Try different things and ask! And, of course, in some positions you can keep pressure on her clitoris during inter-course—or she can—and that can help her maintain arousal too.

In general, though, her arousal level when you start intercourse also determines what you should do. Usually the less aroused she is, the more you start slow and shallow so that you awaken her body and she can progress to wanting more. Do not go for more until she asks for it or shows you that she

> Do not go for more until she asks for it or shows you that she wants it.

wants it by pulling you in further. Once she is very aroused, don't vary things up or tease her. Do the same pressure, the same depth, the same speed until she tells you something else.

Where you may run into problems is that she may take longer to reach orgasm, while you feel like you're ready to burst! That should signal that in the future you need to switch to intercourse later in the process. But there are also steps you can take to help you last longer that don't involve thinking about dead puppies or working through the thirteen times tables in your head. First, pay attention to your breathing. Try to slow it down and keep your breathing deep and deliberate. Since weak pelvic floor muscles may make it more difficult for you to delay ejaculation, try strengthening them ahead of time with Kegel exercises (we tend to think of them for women, but men have a pelvic floor too). Consider using a thicker type of condom to decrease sensation during intercourse.

And depending on how much time (and motivation) you have . . .
the second time around usually lasts longer than the first!

HOW TO DO KEGEL EXERCISES

- Clench the muscles that you would use to stop yourself from urinating or farting.
- Try not to flex other muscles in your abdomen or thighs.
- Hold for three seconds, then release for three seconds.
- Breathe normally (don't hold your breath by reflex).
- Do ten to fifteen at a time, aiming for three sets per day.

At first, isolating the muscles may be easier when lying down. Later on, when you can do them sitting or standing, you can link them to daily activities like brushing your teeth to get in your three sets per day.[5]

HOW TO GET MORE CLITORAL STIMULATION IN THE MAN-ON-TOP POSITION

If she doesn't feel much stimulation when you're on top, try some (or all!) of these tips:

- Have her keep her legs closer together—even try it with your legs outside hers.
- Have her tilt her pelvis up and engage those muscles (like squeezing her butt).
- Change the angle at which you enter her by shifting your body slightly higher up her body.
- Think up-down rather than only in-out. Insert just the tip of your penis, but keep yourself propped up above her, and shift toward her head so that your shaft rubs against her vulva. Then, instead of going in-and-out, try some up-and-down movement.

What If Your Wife Rushes You Along?

What if you're happy to continue for as long as it takes, but it's your wife who constantly tells you it's okay to go ahead and reach orgasm yourself instead of trying to get her to orgasm first?

That's okay—if it happens every now and then. No woman wants to be pressured to have an orgasm, and sometimes she starts sex intending to enjoy it, but there's too much going on in her brain, or her body isn't responding as it usually does for hormonal reasons or something else. If that's the case, she may want the freedom to continue but not to push for her own orgasm. If she says, "I'm enjoying this, and I'm fine with you going ahead," then take the gift!

But this gift should be an *occasional* thing, not an all-the-time thing. Even if she's saying she doesn't mind, and even if she genuinely doesn't mind, this is not a healthy dynamic if it's happening consistently, as we're sure you understand.

A good rule to keep in mind is this simple one: *you can't keep doing the same thing and expect different results.* If she isn't orgasming through what you normally do, then change it up! Start with more kissing and more romance throughout the day. Help her get rid of some of the thoughts swirling in her head. Work on whatever's holding her back. In some of the later sections of this book, we'll help you unpack how some obstacles may be holding her back from the pleasure you both want for her.

Having More Fun Once You're Both Reaching Orgasm!

For many couples, figuring out the orgasm piece for her takes a while. But once you do, you'll likely wonder, "How can we have even more fun?" That's often when couples may try a sex manual showing diagrams of different positions. But looking at diagrams can be tricky if they aren't done tastefully. And using diagrams can feel awkward because it often breaks up sex. You're going all hot and heavy and then you have to stop, pull out the diagram, and readjust. And it can be hard to focus when sex is more like a game of Twister than an intimate experience with your wife.

Let's make this easier. There are only so many ways to have intercourse. Most positions fall into one of four categories:

1. Face-to-face, man on top
2. Face-to-face, woman on top
3. Man facing her back, man on top
4. Man facing her back, woman on top

You can move within these positions to change the pressure, the angle, or the depth you are able to reach. Let's look at some practical ways to change it up so you can experiment without having to consult a manual.

1. Move Your Legs

Wrap your legs around each other, or have her move her legs. Spread them wider, or keep them closer together. Or change where they are in relation to your body. Are they in the air, on the bed, on your shoulders? Try having one of her legs up and one down, and then switch legs to see which feels better. If she's on top, she can try putting one leg forward and one leg back. Also simply changing how far apart her legs are can change the sensation for woman-on-top positions. When you move your legs, you change where your thrusting hits her or how deep you can go.

2. Rotate

If you have sex face-to-face with her on top, you can rotate so you're now on your sides. She can combine this with changing up the position of her legs. Just rolling to the side and having her put one leg on your shoulder puts you in a whole new position! (See how these small changes can make a big difference? They're easy to do, and you don't need to pause and pull out a diagram.)

3. Prop Yourself Up

Change the angle between you and the bed. If you start closer to 90 degrees (sitting up), try moving more toward 180 degrees (lying flat) or vice versa. Or change your position so you're leaning back, holding on to her hands or arms for support. If she's on top, change your position by sitting up. Figure out what combination between you and your wife feels best.

4. Change What Body Part Is Holding Your Weight

If your weight is all on her, try shifting so that your knees, elbows, or your hands support more of your weight. If she's the one on top, try switching from her knees to her feet or to her feet and hands. These kinds of differences can provide a new variation to an old position and make the experience entirely different and new.

No matter what you do, remember one very important rule: you *never ever* hold any of her weight on your penis or be in a situation where her weight could suddenly shift to your penis. A penile fracture is a real thing. It is a medical emergency that requires prompt surgical repair! So be wise, especially with standing positions. Standing positions where you enter her while she is either bending over something (like the side of the bed) or lying on her back on a steady surface are safe. A "Hollywood-style" position where you hold her weight entirely or where she is holding herself up her by wrapping her legs around you can turn bad quickly. No one wants to hear that *snap*.

Ultimately, the amount of variation you have in your sex life is entirely up to the two of you. Just don't lose sight of the main point: it's all about having fun and enjoying each other, not trying to be extreme or win some gymnastics competition.

Even with all these pointers, orgasm may not come instantaneously. We don't want you to see sex as a pass-or-fail test or feel like you're not doing it right. But we do want you to keep aiming for the stars! So remember: orgasm is usually easier in ways other than intercourse. Make sure each sexual encounter has something in it for both of you, even if it's a massage first for her. And keep trying, because she is not broken!

But what if something isn't working right despite your best efforts? Let's turn to that now.

CHAPTER 7

When Sex Isn't Working

We're encouraging you in this book to think of great sex as something that is not only physical but is intimate on every level—physical, emotional, and even spiritual. Though sex is *more* than physical, it still is physical. And, let's be honest, sometimes physical issues can get in the way of having great sex.

With Great Sex, Less Can Be More

Let's start with weight—and we know this isn't an easy conversation. Far too often our society wrongly shames people because of their weight, an error we don't want to repeat. Nevertheless, we can't ignore that excess weight does affect people's experience of sex.

When You're the One with More to Love

Because of the angle of penetration, a husband's obesity can make it difficult for a wife to experience pleasure during intercourse. A large part of what feels good for her is having your pubic bone put pressure on her clitoris with every thrust. But excess weight in that region can prevent the clitoris from getting any stimulation during thrusting. As well, when a man is on the obese end of the spectrum, losing even a bit of weight can give him more usable penile length, harder erections, and more stamina so that sex is just plain better.

It's not that you can't be an awesome lover if you're a bigger guy. You can learn to perform great oral sex. You can learn how her body works and how to make her feel amazing. But women also want to be able to enjoy intercourse, and too much weight can make the man-on-top position especially difficult if she feels like she can't breathe. Obviously there are other positions you can use, but even they can be awkward if extra weight around the midsection gets in the way. If your weight is disrupting your wife's enjoyment of intercourse, consider making some lifestyle changes. It will probably also lead to better sex for you as well, since obesity is correlated with erectile dysfunction as well as lower levels of testosterone (and higher levels of estrogen). And, hey, you'll be healthier overall.

When She's the One with More to Love

What if she's the one who's overweight? First, let's clarify what we mean by "overweight" because it's all too easy to have a double standard here. For instance, Sheila received an email from a woman who asked, "I'm very trim, and my husband loves my body and says he never wants it to change. In fact, he'd prefer not to have children unless I can guarantee I can get back to the same weight. But I really want children, and I don't know what my weight will be afterward. Is this an okay thing to ask of me?"

We even had a man comment on a post once saying that if a woman gains more than twenty-five pounds after her wedding that she's defrauding him and has broken her marriage vows.

If a discussion about your wife's weight is necessary, it must stem from a supportive attitude, not one of entitlement like the men discussed previously. A woman's self-esteem is tied to her appearance far more often than it is for a man. Yet women have more natural reasons for their bodies to change than men do. Having babies means that her stomach will inevitably not be as tight as it was before, even if she goes back to the same weight. She will probably have stretch marks. Her breasts will likely sag a bit, and her stomach will stick out more. Not to put too fine a point on it, but that is the price of carrying your children. Plus, the hormonal changes that happen as we age are more dramatic in women than men, especially around menopause. Your love for your wife's body should not be contingent on her looking like a pinup model or even looking like she did on your wedding night. Instead, have a realistic view of the woman who has stood beside you and (potentially) bore your children. One husband at a marriage conference we spoke at had the right idea. When his wife worried that her body wasn't back to what it was after their four kids, he told her, "You should be proud of your body; you worked hard for it!"

That being said, there is a difference between typical weight gain (postpartum and with age) and weight gain that carries health risks. Whether the issue is with you or your wife or with both of you, ignoring the problem won't help anybody. Just remember to address the issue in terms of health rather than appearance, and have compassion on yourself and your wife as you commit to being healthier.

We know that weight management comes down to two things: how much goes into the body and how much you burn with activity, mediated by your metabolism and body type. For some people, losing weight is simply easier than it is for others. But regardless of what category you fall into, having a positive body image and strong self-esteem makes losing weight easier than if you feel bad about yourself.[1] Don't berate yourself for not being able to lose weight; celebrate who you are and look forward to what you'll be able to do as you get healthier. When it comes to your wife, boosting her confidence can make it easier for her to lose weight;

> Your job is to love your wife now, not when she loses thirty pounds.

criticizing her will make it more difficult. Your job is to love your wife now, not when she loses thirty pounds. But even as you love and accept her, you can still incorporate healthy habits into your life, such as taking walks every night after dinner, taking it upon yourself to cook healthy meals, or taking your wife out dancing every week.

Sex Shouldn't Hurt

Piper and John had done everything right. They had aimed to save sex for marriage, and they made it to their wedding night both virgins. The few big make-out sessions they'd enjoyed before marriage were often followed by feelings of intense guilt on Piper's part, and she would declare a fast from kissing for forty days. Yet even Piper was counting down the days until their wedding—and their wedding night.

After the dancing and the speeches and the confetti, they ended up in their hotel room, feeling awkward. They kissed a bit. They took off their clothes. But when they tried to have intercourse, they couldn't. Piper was so tense and so tight that it hurt too much.

It took the couple four years before penetration was possible—four years of trying and failing, four years of frustration and tears. They used other ways to bring John to orgasm, though Piper could never quite let John help her.

A few years into this struggle, Piper started seeing a physiotherapist who specialized in pelvic floor issues. She learned exercises to do, and the physiotherapist stretched her. Finally, after a lot of effort, penetration was possible, and they had their first child. But those years of frustration left their toll on the couple.

Their story is not unique. In the Bare Marriage survey Sheila conducted, she found that 22.6 percent of women had experienced vaginismus or other conditions that make intercourse painful (such as vulvodynia or lichen sclerosus), and 6.8 percent of women had such bad sexual pain that penetration was impossible.[2]

Vaginismus, or sexual pain, isn't something women deliberately cause, and it isn't a sign that they don't want you or don't love you. It doesn't mean they're psychologically scarred or necessarily have abuse in their past. Vaginismus is a physical condition where the muscles at the opening of the vagina (generally the first one and a half inches) stay tense. Think of it like a giant muscle spasm that you can't relax.

It seems to be a multifaceted issue that can be impacted by stress, bowel issues, posture—basically anything that affects the pelvic floor. But it also seems to have some roots in beliefs we grow up with, because researchers have known for a long time that being religiously conservative is a risk factor for vaginismus. In our surveys, we tried to pinpoint what it was about being religiously conservative that contributed to sexual pain, and we found several markers. One was the obligation sex message: wives who believe before they are married that they are obligated to give their husband sex when he wants it once they are married are 37 percent more likely to experience vaginismus.

Another predictor of vaginismus is how the first sexual experience plays out. If women have had sex only with their now-husband, they are 25.1 percent more likely to have primary sexual pain if their first consensual sexual experience was on or after the wedding night. Why? We think it has everything to do with arousal. Women who have sex on their wedding night aren't always aroused when it happens. But if they have sex before marriage? We believe women are much more likely to be aroused and *want* sex. We're not arguing for sex before marriage; only that this evidence gives us even more indication that it's vitally important not to rush through to intercourse as soon as you have that wedding ring on. Instead, work through the natural sexual progression cycle so you're sure she's aroused!

How to Treat Sexual Pain

For most women, pelvic floor physiotherapy is a large part of their recovery process for vaginismus. A pelvic floor physiotherapist will likely do some stretching exercises with her, give her exercises to do at home, and give a set of vaginal trainers that helps her slowly stretch.[3]

You can help speed her recovery by helping her let go of any beliefs she has that may be making vaginismus worse. If she believes the obligation sex message, for instance, then not being able to have intercourse is likely causing her a boatload of guilt, exacerbating the condition. Treat her with grace. Make sex something that is still wonderful for her by showing her that she can still enjoy her body even without intercourse. There are many ways to have fun without penetration—focus on those! Reassure her that you will figure this out together, that this is not *her* problem but your problem *together*, and that you know she isn't intentionally "depriving you." What she has is involuntary, so it's an "in sickness and in health" issue.

What about the Postpartum Phase?

Often new dads have the six-week doctor's checkup circled on their calendar because they see it as the green light for sex again! But what if six weeks comes and goes and she's still not cleared? Or what if there's still pain? Sheila's study found that 26.7 percent of women experienced significant pain with postpartum sex. For some women, vaginismus can develop after childbirth, exacerbated either by new scar tissue or a traumatic birth experience.

If your wife experiences sexual pain after childbirth, treat this as an issue that you will get through together, rather than as a disappointment to you. A pelvic floor physiotherapist can often help her recover from any birth trauma, and with treatment and time, most women do recover. But if you push sex too early when it's painful or make her feel guilty for how long she's taking to recover, you may worsen her postpartum problems while creating a whole host of new ones. If she believes you value your pleasure over her pain, that can't help but affect how she feels about sex.

When we were first married, Sheila suffered from vaginismus—and from guilt. She felt she was depriving me of the sex life I had waited for and dreamed about before we were married, so she decided to push through for my sake. I wish I had realized that was what was going on, but I had no clue. I was too selfish to see it at the time. Because she'd been told that men feel love through sex, she was afraid of losing my love. So she assured me we should keep trying despite her pain, and we did. I thought her pain was lessening. I found out later that Sheila was simply getting better at masking it. Of everything in my life, this is my deepest regret. Not just that I hurt the one I love but that I didn't even know how much I was hurting her—because I should have known. I should have taken the focus off me entirely and focused on her. Instead, her healing took longer than it should have and left emotional scars that took years to mend.

Telling a woman that the way you feel loved is to do something that causes her pain is a traumatic message. Love does not require someone else's pain. Listen to this anguished woman's words:

My husband and I used to enjoy sexual intimacy and never had any problems—until after the birth of our first child. When we tried intercourse, it was extremely painful. We have tried unsuccessfully several times since then. The sexual dysfunction exposed underlying issues in our relationship that we have not been able to repair, and we are heading toward separation. My husband has a very fundamentalistic view of the Bible, and I think he would like me to suffer through the pain and fulfill my duty for his sake. That duty mentality completely kills any arousal and does not help fix my problem of pain. I just can't do it. That's not to say I am not open to other ways of being sexually intimate, it is just that this hostility between us makes it seem impossible to do with a sincere heart.

It is interesting to me that when it is my body that got injured during birth (pelvic organ prolapse) and my body that now experiences pain during intercourse, he acts as if he is the only one hurting. I know he loves me, but I feel so objectified. The fact that my husband wants me to have sex with him despite intense pain disgusts me, and I really question who I chose to marry.

Don't be like this woman's husband. And don't be like I used to be. Love your wife as your own body—and that means that her pain matters more than your pleasure.

When Sex Isn't Working for *You*

In junior high you couldn't keep it down. But what happens if now you can't keep it up?

First of all, don't panic! It happens sometimes. Male sexuality isn't always as automatic as it is portrayed to be. It may be that you are tired or stressed. Since there is a psychological component to erections, getting freaked out and nervous about your ability to get one may make things worse. The first step is to relax and enjoy each other in other ways and simply try again later.

If issues persist, know that you are not alone. Erectile dysfunction (ED) is common. A multinational study of men ages twenty to seventy-five found an overall incidence of 16 percent.[4] It increases with age, from 8 percent in men age twenty to thirty, up to 37 percent in men over seventy. So there is no reason to feel embarrassed about seeking help—in fact, you should.

Erections are caused by blood flowing to the penis, which depends on good circulation. The onset of erectile dysfunction can be an indicator of possible coronary artery disease, even in men with few other risk factors.[5] Diabetes, high blood pressure, and hypothyroidism are also strongly linked to erectile dysfunction. Going to the doctor may not be high on the list of activities you enjoy, but you need to talk to a physician not only to deal with the problem but to rule out other health issues as well.

Anything that hinders circulation or decreases one's heart rate can also lead to erectile dysfunction, including smoking and alcohol use or taking certain medications. Trying to be healthier by cutting back on substances that can harm you is a good start, as well as talking to your doctor about any medications you are taking.

When we think of erectile dysfunction, we usually picture older guys in late-night commercials talking about little blue pills. But there's another face of erectile dysfunction that surprises many people: it's a guy in his twenties or thirties whose sexual response has been disrupted by pornography. And the little blue pill isn't the answer because it's not a circulatory problem. It's a mental one.

Erectile Dysfunction with Porn Use

In younger men, sexual dysfunction is highly correlated with porn use. In our survey, men who never use porn are 2.4 times less likely to have erectile dysfunction than men who use it daily. Porn trains your brain to become aroused by an image or video rather than by relationship, so then when you're with your wife, she can't provide enough excitement. One of the lures of porn is that it's always different. With an alcohol addiction, an alcoholic eventually develops tolerance: the same amount of alcohol doesn't give the same buzz, and so more is needed. With porn, it's not that you need *more*, it's that you need *different*—different bodies, different actions, different scenarios. That's why users often seek out porn that is more and more extreme. As the search for "different" and "new" intensifies, guys seek images that they initially would never have wanted to see.

We'll talk about porn at greater length later in the book, but let us say now that porn use will not help your sex life; it will only harm it.

But porn isn't the only psychological cause of erectile dysfunction. Stress, fatigue, relationship issues, and other problems can also contribute. Talking through these issues with a licensed counselor can be invaluable in those cases.

Delayed Ejaculation

Delayed ejaculation—when men take an abnormally long time to reach orgasm or never reach orgasm at all—can also mess with sexual satisfaction. Again, delayed ejaculation is highly linked to porn use. In our survey, men who use porn daily were 4.1 times more likely to have delayed ejaculation than men who never use porn. Because the sexual response cycle has been associated with pornography and masturbation, you may find it difficult to reach orgasm with less intense stimulation. The quick solution: quit the pornography and masturbation so your body gets back to the point where being with your wife is enough for you. But porn is not always the issue. There are other causes of delayed ejaculation, including certain medications. In that case, talk to your doctor.

Premature Ejaculation

Premature ejaculation is a condition where a man orgasms faster than normal and faster than he or his partner would like. Typically, that means less than one minute after vaginal penetration, which can be distressing to both him and his wife. The biggest challenge for couples is that men are often too embarrassed to seek help, which is a shame because psychological and medical treatments are available.

For some men, the solution may be as simple as wearing thicker condoms. Other men have benefitted from using the pause-squeeze technique or, if that's too intense for you, the start-and-stop technique. Finally, there are medications your doctor may be able to prescribe if these techniques haven't worked.

The Pause-Squeeze Technique

- Engage in sexual activity until you are close to ejaculation.
- Stop and squeeze (or have your wife squeeze) your penis firmly where the head joins the shaft until the urge to ejaculate passes and your erection starts to diminish. This should not be painful. If anything hurts, stop immediately.
- Repeat as necessary. The point is to train you to recognize the signals in your body that occur before you orgasm.

The Start-and-Stop Technique

- Engage in sexual activity until you are close to ejaculation.
- Stop once you feel you are close to orgasm.
- Wait until the urge to ejaculate passes, then resume.
- Repeat this three times with the goal of having an orgasm on the fourth time.
- Repeat as necessary. It can take weeks before you see a difference.

Can You Have a Sex Life Even with Sexual Dysfunction?

Sexual dysfunction can take a real emotional toll, but your beliefs about sexuality can make the situation easier or more difficult. Don't let shame or embarrassment stop you from seeking help when it is readily available. Similarly, having the restricted view that sex is only intercourse can make facing erectile dysfunction psychologically devastating. Instead, remember what we said in chapter 1: great sex is more than just intercourse; it is all sexual activity the two of you do together, with the aim of mutual satisfaction. Focus on a more holistic view of sex, giving each other satisfaction in the ways you can while you work through these issues with trusted professionals.

When You Have No Libido

What if it's not that sex isn't working, but rather it's that sex isn't happening? You don't particularly crave sex, and it never really crosses your mind. While men are usually portrayed as having insatiable sex drives, 25.6 percent of men in our survey think they aren't having sex enough, but they aren't really bothered by it. Another 3.7 percent of men feel pressure from their wives to have more sex.

When you're the one with the lower libido, you may think a low frequency of sex is fine. But first, remember that it may not be fine for your wife. Second, since sex is an important part of a healthy relationship with you wife, its absence jeopardizes intimacy. Finally, it may also indicate that something else is going on. If you rarely feel the desire for sex, or if it takes a significant amount of time to get aroused when you start making love, have a physician check your testosterone levels. Many guys have told us, "We spent years fighting over my lack of libido until I finally had my testosterone levels checked. I was on the low end, and after I started getting shots, suddenly my libido returned. And so did our sex life!" And they almost all end their comments the same way: "I wish we had checked years earlier."

In other cases, your low libido may be caused by other elements of your relationship, or even by things that happened in your past that are affecting you now. Let's leave the physical side of sex behind and turn now to how the emotional aspects of sex can impact pleasure and libido for both of you.

EMOTIONAL COMPANIONSHIP AND CLOSENESS

The Greatest Need

We have a running joke when we speak at FamilyLife Canada marriage conferences. We invariably give the sex talk—the last talk of the day—which follows right after the communication talk. As we make our way to the podium, we always remind the audience, "Remember, communication comes before sex!"

And it's true. Great sex flows out of a loving relationship and is also a tangible, physical expression of that relationship. For your sex life to be everything you want as a couple, the relationship itself has to be solid. In this section, we'd like to explore emotional intimacy as it relates to sex. To sum it up bluntly: you have to like each other for sex to be great. You have to be good friends who want to spend time together *in general* before spending time together *in bed* can rock your world.

Research has shown that the better your relationship is outside the bedroom, the better it will be inside it.[1] Couples who feel happier in marriage overall also tend to feel satisfied with the closeness they experience in the bedroom—and that is true even more so for women.

Feeling like sex is something that brings you closer together is largely dependent on feeling close in the nonsexual aspects of your relationship.

That's one of the reasons, incidentally, why saving sex for marriage can be such a good thing. When delaying gratification during

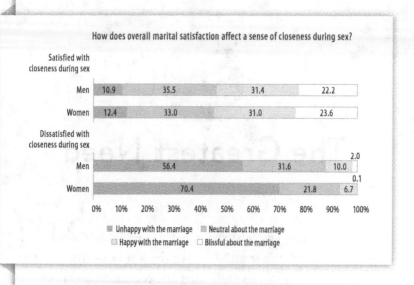

How does overall marital satisfaction affect a sense of closeness during sex?

Satisfied with closeness during sex

Men	10.9	35.5	31.4	22.2
Women	12.4	33.0	31.0	23.6

Dissatisfied with closeness during sex

Men	56.4	31.6	10.0	2.0
Women	70.4	21.8	6.7	0.1

0%   10%   20%   30%   40%   50%   60%   70%   80%   90%   100%

■ Unhappy with the marriage   ▨ Neutral about the marriage
▢ Happy with the marriage   ▢ Blissful about the marriage

your dating months and years, you naturally spend the time doing activities other than just making out. But for many couples, these relationship-building pursuits fall by the wayside after they get married and can "do it." Sex takes over as their primary way of experiencing closeness.

Resist that temptation. Couples who focus too much on orgasm and not enough on friendship don't tend to have the most satisfying sex lives in the long run.[2] Instead, the emotional and physical aspects of your relationship should reinforce each other, making sex—and your marriage—better.

Sex, especially for women, involves being vulnerable. She can't be vulnerable with someone she doesn't love and trust. If there's tension in the bedroom because it's taking a while to get things right or you're struggling with libido differences or other issues, then work on your friendship. Being able to laugh together outside the bedroom helps calm the situation so you can talk more easily about these tension-fraught issues.

Besides, it never hurts to turn up the fun quotient in your marriage. A few years after our wedding, after working out some of our earlier difficulties around sex, we watched a movie where a fun-loving couple added the words *in bed* to the end of the messages inside Chinese fortune cookies. That gives the fortune an entirely new meaning! Now whenever we visit a Chinese restaurant, we eagerly crack open the cookies the instant the bill comes. We've saved hundreds over the years. Here are just a few (you'll have to add the words *in bed* yourself):

- You have many ideas and the energy to put them into action.
- You have unusual equipment for success. Use it wisely.
- It is time to help a friend in need.
- You tend to draw out the talent in others.
- Your present plans are going to succeed.
- Be content with your lot. One cannot be first in everything.
- You possess an excellent imagination.
- Use your talents. That's what they are intended for.
- Fight for it. You will come out on top.
- You work best when meticulous attention to detail is called for.
- If your feet are firmly planted, you cannot be moved.
- You can't expect to be a lucky dog if you're always growling.

No matter what mood we're in, if we find a "good" fortune, we smile. Having these little jokes that can turn up at odd times throughout the week makes you laugh together and reminds you that you are connected in a unique way to this person—and only to this person. It's a whole different kind of fun.

Developing Common Hobbies

Spending low-key time together bolsters fun. But that's not always easy. The activities that one person considers fun don't always turn the other's crank. Often, after marriage, you settle into your hobbies and she settles into hers. Some couples soon find that the only things they do together are logistical: grocery shopping, errands, caring for children.

That's what happened to a couple who are very important to us—we'll call them Tanya and Mike. They were passionately in love when they married. Their physical attraction was solid, but unfortunately they had little else in common other than the children who came in quick succession. Early in their relationship they started to lead separate lives. Tanya stayed home with the children all day and then in the evening would occasionally convince Mike to watch them so she could go out for a girls' night. Mike drowned himself in video games. They didn't even eat together most nights since Mike would eat in front of the computer, and Tanya often ate with the kids. Not surprisingly, their marriage ended after less than a decade.

What is surprising is the number of couples who think this kind of distance is inevitable. Nonsense! Tanya and Mike did not have to drift apart; they could have drifted together if they had made an effort to stay connected.

We live in the Great White North, where every winter the ritual of taking kids to hockey practice begins anew. We never participated in this ritual since we were blessed with daughters who didn't particularly like hockey, but friends of ours had three boys who did. So naturally they had three schedules for games and practices. Driving the boys to practice soaked up their life.

One year they decided that they'd divide and conquer. Lori would get Tuesdays and Thursdays, and Greg would take Mondays and Wednesdays so that they would each have two evenings off a week. Sounded like bliss!

But by the end of the second week, they realized they had spent no time together all week. So the next week they ditched that plan and started going to practices *together* two nights a week. They'd bring blankets and thermoses of hot chocolate and sit in the bleachers watching their boys, talking about the future, and generally catching up. They realized that shivering together was better than relaxing apart. Spending time together matters, and sometimes that means undertaking endeavors you normally wouldn't.

About eight years ago Sheila and I watched *The Big Year*, a movie with Steve Martin, Owen Wilson, and Jack Black, about competitive bird watching. (You didn't read that wrong. There is such a thing as competitive bird watching.) It turns out that we live about forty minutes from one of the ten best birding areas in Canada, and we had watched the film just before spring migration. Inspired, we equipped ourselves with binoculars and headed out to hunt for warblers. I was instantly hooked! Birding has become something of an obsession for me. I keep lists of what I have seen and will go to great lengths to add to those lists. Sheila never caught the bug in the same way. Strangely, she doesn't find it enthralling to sit in a marsh at five o'clock in the morning getting bitten by mosquitoes in order to see a least bittern. But she does go with me if the terrain and timing are more reasonable. For her, it's not about adding birds to her list; it's about enjoying a walk in the woods with her husband.

What she loves to do is ballroom dancing! When she first suggested it, I hesitated, and not only because I'm not a good dancer. I also felt that, even when you are a good dancer, it looks kind of silly. But I knew it mattered to her, and I dutifully went to lessons.

Just my making the effort meant so much to Sheila. As we've practiced, we've become decent. Now when we're on vacation, we can dance to the bands—as long as they don't play a samba. We still can't do a samba. But there's something awfully romantic about holding each other and moving to music, even if you are worried you'll look silly.

Participating in each other's hobbies can change the dynamic of your relationship. Embrace something because your wife likes it, and you may find that you like it too. When you spend time together and invest in each other's lives, navigating the bumps in a relationship becomes easier. The friendship you have built gives you strength to draw from. But if your relationship is only about family logistics, then you not only lack that strength, you may also find problems magnified because you feel so disconnected.

Respecting Bedtimes

Spending time together during the day builds connection, but spending time together at night builds real intimacy. Our evening routines matter. We may not think of exhaustion as a marriage issue, but it is. When we're tired, we don't have time or energy to pay attention to our spouses because we're so desperate to relax or rest. And it's not only the amount of sleep that's important but also the timing of that sleep. At marriage conferences, I often tell the guys that there is a time and a place where sex is most likely to happen. At that time of day, if you aren't in that place, you can't complain if sex isn't happening. And that time and place tends to be *in the bedroom when you are going to bed*. Like Colonel Mustard in the library with the candlestick—*it's the husband in the bedroom with the wife.*

Did you know that baby-boomer couples used to all go to bed at the same time? It was right after the ten o'clock news or after Johnny Carson's monologue on *The Tonight Show*. There wasn't much choice in TV land, so when those shows were done, *you* were done. But today mothing magically ends at 10:30 p.m. or at 11:10 p.m. to tell us, "That's it. Nothing more to see here. May as well turn in." All too often couples are separately on screens in the evening, and then they head to bed when they're exhausted— often at different times.

How can you keep a sex life alive if you scatter at night? Sheila and I love chatting in bed or even while getting ready for bed. Spending the last few moments of the day holding each other is an important bedtime ritual. And we're not just talking about sex either. Sure, it's going to be harder to connect sexually if you're not in bed at the same time. But it's harder to connect *at all*.

Count backward eight hours from when the one who has to get up earliest has to rise. That's when you should be getting to sleep. Now count backward another forty-five minutes or so. That's when the bedtime routine should start: sharing a cup of tea together, having a shower together, brushing your teeth, climbing into bed, and reading a book for a few minutes. If the kids wake you up at 6:15 a.m., then you need to be asleep by 10:15 p.m. That means you start your bedtime routine by 9:30 p.m. Yes, you'll miss out on some video game time, and you may have time for only one Netflix episode. But trust us: it's worth it.

Going Deeper

Okay, that heading got you, didn't it? But here we're talking about going *emotionally* deeper. If sex is the culmination of your relationship, then if that relationship is shallow, sex will also seem shallow. Your wife doesn't want only your body, she wants your heart too. That means we have to be able to communicate and share on a deep level.

John Powell, author of *Why Am I Afraid to Tell You Who I Am?*, describes communication as having five levels, starting out shallow and growing deeper, like this:[3]

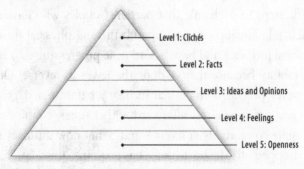

Level 1: Clichés
Level 2: Facts
Level 3: Ideas and Opinions
Level 4: Feelings
Level 5: Openness

Intimacy increases with each level because each one requires more vulnerability. You can talk in clichés with someone you don't even know: "Nice day, isn't it?" Similarly, talking about facts—where many couples spend most of their time—doesn't require any vulnerability: "Johnny has band practice tomorrow at three, and someone has to pick him up afterward. Can you do that on the way home from work?" Sharing opinions isn't that scary either: "I think my new supervisor is out to get me. She never smiles and nothing I do is right!"

But it's in the deeper levels of communication that we become vulnerable. That's where we build the strongest connections by sharing feelings: "I'm worried that my boss is going to think that the supervisor is right. I'm scared I might lose my job." Or when we dig deep to be completely open: "I want to feel like I'm making a difference, but lately it seems like no one even notices my contributions. What if God is disappointed in me too?"

Imagine a marriage where all the communication is at the facts level. The couple may talk a lot, but it won't help them know each other better. Will intimacy improve if they start sharing opinions? Yes, marginally. But opinions still tend to be safe since you're sharing only your thoughts. It's feelings that reveal what's really going on inside us—our wants, our needs, our dreams.

Many couples never learn to communicate comfortably at levels 4 and 5. And often the level of emotional intimacy we've reached when we become sexually involved is the level we stay at—unless we take specific steps to overcome that barrier. Couples who have sex early in their relationship can end up substituting physical intimacy for emotional intimacy and have a hard time progressing into emotional vulnerability because they've done the levels in reverse. Or couples who never practiced emotional intimacy before marriage may feel stuck and never progress afterward. Other times, couples may have lived quite comfortably at levels 4 and 5, but now intimacy seems to have dropped off. Maybe distance has crept into the relationship, and they don't feel safe being vulnerable anymore, or maybe they have gotten so busy that they don't have time to communicate.

Vulnerability is the key to feeling close. We don't get to communication levels 4 and 5 with many people, and we bond most with those with whom we do. Make sure, then, that one of those people is your wife.

Many men have trouble reaching levels 4 and 5 because we aren't comfortable talking in emotional language, probably due to societal conditioning. Marc Alan Schelske, in his book *The Wisdom of Your Heart*, points out that our society unfortunately allows men only one "negative" emotion: anger. When, as a boy, you're discouraged from showing emotions like fear or insecurity or anxiety, or when you're told that God doesn't like those feelings, then as a man you'll have a hard time even naming what you feel because you've been running from those feelings your whole life. It's hard to share what you can't acknowledge.

Many of us don't even realize that sharing is important. We're often told that wives need to be able to talk to us, and so we think we've done our job if we dutifully listen. But for communication to build intimacy, it must be a two-way street. Wives don't just want us to hear their hearts, they want to hear ours too.

Different personalities can also make emotional conversations tricky. One newlywed couple we've mentored encountered this early in their marriage. Callie is a bubbly extrovert, and Jonathan is the strong, silent type. One Saturday morning Callie made Jonathan an amazing breakfast of waffles, which he appreciated very much. Then she needed help with a work project—building a sample diorama of *Romeo and Juliet* for the English class she was teaching. Together they put the finishing touches on the balcony scene. Afterward she suggested taking a walk, and he held her hand as he enjoyed strolling with his bride in the stillness of the autumn air.

Jonathan came home feeling awesome. He'd had a delicious breakfast. He'd been a superhero for Callie, helping her complete her work. And he'd spent quality time with her in nature, something he knew was important to her.

Callie, on the other hand, returned from that walk almost in tears, wondering what she had done wrong. Jonathan had barely spoken at breakfast. He had worked on the diorama but barely said a word. She figured he must have resented having to spend his Saturday morning on her work. And then for the walk, he'd barely said anything either! She knew he didn't like walks as much as she did. He must have been really upset that the whole day had become about her. When she finally asked him about it, she was blown away when he said he felt it had been one of the best days of their marriage!

How did they see this day in such different ways? Callie is an extrovert with a strong feeling preference, while Jonathan is an introvert with a strong thinking preference. To Jonathan, spending time together in silence is a great way to grow intimacy; for Callie, time together in silence can feel like important things are going unsaid and can make her worry there's something wrong.

Callie often has trouble getting Jonathan to share his thoughts and feelings with her. She finds if she asks, "How was your day?" he tends to give very short answers. "Fine." "Not too bad." In Jonathan's mind, he doesn't want to burden her with his worries and prefers to put work in the background when he gets home. She sometimes feels like she doesn't know what's going on with him.

So she tries another approach and asks, "What did you do today?" But that's a tricky one to answer. What does she want to know? *"Well, I had five client meetings, and my boss wanted to talk about the upcoming quarterly report, and I went to the bank over lunch . . ."* It isn't that Jonathan didn't want to communicate with Callie. It's that he didn't have a way to do so that felt natural.

Sheila and I have developed a habit that can overcome some of these hesitancies and help get to the heart of emotion, and it takes only about ten minutes a day. Here's how it works: every day, share with each other the time today that you felt God working through you, felt the most energized, or felt the most "in the groove." And then share the time you felt the most defeated, exhausted, or discouraged. That's easier than answering the question, "What did you do today?" Sharing two snapshots of your day lets your spouse understand your heart and gives you insight too.

Learning to go to deeper levels of communication can feel awkward and strange. Having a daily ritual like this high-low exercise makes talking at these deeper levels easier than expecting those conversations to spontaneously occur. It's the kind of thing Jonathan can easily share with Callie. Now he even watches for moments that he wants to tell her about. And Callie can feel like she knows what's going on in her husband's heart, even if he never becomes a big talker.

Keep Everything in Perspective

Couples often have highs and lows in their sex lives. Sometimes you'll have the higher sex drive, and sometimes she will. Rarely does your sex life have the same frequency, the same intensity, and the same physical rush for decades. Yet those who have a strong friendship find these ups and downs much easier to navigate. When you're friends, sex drives return faster. You want to give to each other. And when problems pop up, addressing them head-on is easier when the stress level in your marriage is already low.

So make this promise to yourself: even if we go through a sexual rut, I will do my best to increase the fun in our relationship and stay emotionally close.

Commit to finding new ways of laughing together and sharing together, and problems you have in the bedroom will diminish. And when sex doesn't go as you hoped, tell her, "Let's laugh about it and keep trying because we have years to improve!"

And while you're at it, order Chinese.

CHAPTER 9

Sex Sorta Begins in the Kitchen (But Not Why You Think)

Have you ever heard "sex begins in the kitchen"? It's not suggesting that we should get creative with whipping cream but that doing the dishes is a good method to get women to warm up. *Guys, if you want her to have sex with you, you had better pick up a dish towel!*

But does that honestly work? And if so, isn't it a bit manipulative? The answer to both is "it depends." Specifically, it depends on your motivation.

Does Doing Housework Turn Her On?

When Sheila asks on her Facebook page what best gets women in the mood, what they usually say is for husbands to do some form of housework. This often gets guys' attention. Since guys tend to have the higher libido, "How do I get her to have sex more?" is a common question. And many higher-libido guys respond as you'd expect. If they think cleaning the living room will result in action in the bedroom, you can pretty much guarantee they will pull out that vacuum cleaner!

This message of "Do X so she'll do Y" is pretty widespread. But when it's presented this way—*What can I do to make you want sex?*—then the emphasis is in the wrong place, and it can backfire big-time, as this woman explains:

> I am struggling to make my list of what makes me feel in the mood. I feel like my suggestions are treated as a magic formula to make me excited about having sex. If I ask my husband to be more helpful, then I might notice that he's washing dishes or helping out more. But if that doesn't result in enthusiastic sex, then he's resentful and irritated. He frequently compliments me on my looks, but it always feels like a prelude to getting something in bed. I don't even want to suggest anything else because if he starts doing it, he'll be expecting something in return. Maybe that's not really true, but it feels that way, so it's hard to know how to move forward.

If you compliment her on her looks as a ploy to get sex, she'll never really believe you think she's pretty. If you help around the house because you hope to get sex, she'll be left feeling that you actually expect her to do all the housework. If you do things with the expectation that you will get sex, you paint those acts of service as something she should be grateful for, as if you're going the extra mile instead of acting like a true partner in the marriage. Kindness isn't kindness if you're doing it to get something. It's manipulation. She will see right through your ulterior motive, and that will not boost her libido.

This "X leads to Y" thinking is problematic on many levels. It depicts sex as something *you* naturally want but she needs to be bribed into because she doesn't really want it. If women hear this again and again, is it any wonder many have low libidos? But worse than that, it paints sex as transactional instead of relational. Women are trying to tell us (if we will listen) that they consider housework a turn-on *if we approach it correctly*. When a man does dishes because he's a responsible, decent human being who wants to be a true partner in the marriage, she will feel supported and valued, which will help her desire him more. She will want sex more because she feels as if she has a true partner and because she's not exhausted, not because she feels she has to "pay" him for his good behavior.

> She will want sex more because she feels as if she has a true partner and because she's not exhausted, not because she feels she has to "pay" him for his good behavior.

Do you see the difference? He isn't doing dishes to get sex. He's doing dishes because *that's what he should do*. He's an adult. He eats. He dirties dishes. So he does dishes because he's a decent, mature, responsible human being—and women tend to be attracted to decent, mature, responsible human beings!

But an even greater threat to women's libidos is how a couple handles emotional labor and mental load. Sheila wrote a series on her blog that resonated tremendously with women, who felt this described perfectly why their libidos had tanked. Not sure what emotional labor and mental load mean? Let's paint a picture with a couple we'll call Sandra and Mark.

It's a beautiful Saturday morning, and Mark has blessed Sandra with a morning all to herself while he takes the kids. Sandra's up early, excited about her outing. As she leaves the house, she says to Mark, "Remember to get the clothes out of the dryer when the load is done."

While she's gone, Mark feeds the kids a fun pancake breakfast, and then they head out on a bike ride. When Sandra gets home, the kids are energetic and happy, and Mark is beaming.

Sandra smiles, relaxed from her morning, and starts to make lunch when she notices that the birthday present for her son Brian's friend is still sitting on the kitchen counter, unwrapped. And they have to leave in two hours. "That's okay," Sandra thinks, sighing. "I'll just do it."

As she fetches the wrapping paper, she sees Brian's science fair project on the dining room table, untouched. "Didn't Mark get Brian to work on the science fair project? We won't have time to work on it tomorrow, and it's due Monday!" Then another thought occurs: "What about Janie practicing piano?"

Now they're under the gun because Sandra was planning on staying with Brian at the party this afternoon. So, in the next two hours, Brian needs to make headway on the project and Janie needs to practice piano. Sandra starts ordering the kids around, and they get grumpy. Mark tells her to calm down, but Sandra feels the clock ticking.

After much protest, the kids comply, begrudgingly, as Mark heads outside on the riding lawn mower, listening to podcasts. Sandra goes to grab her jeans and realizes they're not folded on the bed. Are they still in the dryer? Uh oh! All of Mark's work shirts were in the dryer. If he didn't pull them out when the dryer was done, then she'll need to do extra ironing. She checks the dryer. Yep. The laundry is still there.

Mark's done mowing the lawn, and he calls out, "Oh, hon, I forgot to tell you. My sister called this morning. She wants to know what venue we should book for Mom and Dad's fortieth anniversary party."

"What did you tell her?" Sandra asks.

"I told her you'd call her back."

"But they're your parents," Sandra thinks. Anger starts showing on her face. Mark can't figure out what's going on but then says, "Oh, is this about the laundry? Look, I'm sorry. I just forgot."

And then Sandra bursts. It wasn't just the laundry. It was the unwrapped birthday present and the homework and the piano. It was everything.

"But if you needed me to do all that," Mark says, "you should have given me a list."

Sandra feels the frustration rise, even as she tries to stuff it down. *Is it so bad to wish that I didn't have to write him a list? Is it wrong to want him to know some of this stuff without having to be told?* The present was right in the middle of the kitchen where he had made pancakes. They had talked about the science fair project last night at dinner—it was all over the dining room table. Janie had been practicing for weeks, and the Tuesday recital was circled with stars on the calendar. Was it so unreasonable that she wanted Mark to think of some of these things too, without being reminded?

Mark tries to calm her down. "Honey, you're overreacting. We can get all of this done later. You don't have to go crazy now."

But when is this magical "later" when everything is supposed to get done? Why didn't Mark realize that their schedule was tight this weekend? Why did she always carry the mental calendar?

That's mental load—always feeling like you have to carry everyone's calendar and the family to-do list in your head, always remembering what everyone else needs to get done.

Studies have shown that women tend to carry far more mental load than men do.[1] Certainly men may be stressed at work (as may women), but paid work often comes with distinct "off time." Carrying mental load for the family never ends. And here's something interesting: you know how we always assume that women are better multitaskers than men? It turns out they're not![2] *They simply have more practice at it.* Women aren't innately able to multitask better than men, but women usually assume more responsibility for all those little tasks that go into running a family. They get good at multitasking because they have to.

And it's exhausting.

Having a million things in your head all the time—the piano recital and having to stay on top of your kids' practicing, the ironing, the science fair project, the birthday party, the homework, the housework, the grocery lists—makes it hard to relax enough for libido to kick in. We've often wondered whether it's even true that men have a higher libido than women or whether women simply carry so many thoughts in their heads all the time that sexual desire simply gets pushed out!

As Sandra thought, "Is it wrong to want him to know some of this stuff without having to be told?" If she has to write him a list, then she still has to remember everything, to organize everything. If it's still in her head, *it's still her responsibility*. If you want her to have more of a libido, then take some of the responsibilities. Own some of the big household tasks so that she never has to think about them.

This concept has been so helpful for us as a couple. Instead of dividing up what chores we each should do every week, we each simply permanently "own" a different part of the household work. I own planning for vacations, so Sheila never thinks about where we're going, whether the passports need to be renewed, what reservations need to be made, when down payments are due. She only has to pack her clothes when it's time to go (there's no way she'd let me take that on). I own the finances, so she doesn't have to worry about charity or budgeting or when the scary notices from the IRS arrive. But she owns the cooking and the meal planning, and I never have to think about what we will eat. We each own our areas so that the mental load for those areas is completely off our spouse.

What does that leave? Breathing room. And when you have time to breathe, then libido can grow. So instead of trying to find a magic formula to boost her libido, put your effort into taking on more of the mental load and responsibilities at home so that she feels supported.

Sometimes, though, the reason that mental load isn't equally shared is because of deep feelings of inadequacy in one of you. One man left this comment on Sheila's blog, explaining why the negative sexual dynamic in their marriage started:

Married for eleven years, I grew up as a Christian, as did my wife. I studied theology independently and even led a small group. My wife was my rock, not vice versa. I leaned on her strength, and she didn't have mine to lean on. I was emotionally unstable, easily angered or triggered into defensiveness or frustration and withdrawal. I was unpredictable and unstable. Even after work, she didn't know if I was going to yell at the kids or be happy. I struggled with deep issues of feeling like I would never be good enough. We had an imbalanced sex drive because I would only do things around the house to earn "brownie points" with my wife. I acted just like the kids did, and she was consequently attracted to me in the same way (she wasn't). The conversation of sex came up constantly, and always in the context of her not meeting my needs, followed by my moping and self-pity, like a little boy who's begging Mommy to fix his booboo. It was loving, pity sex, not mutually passionate, erotic sex. My wife was overwhelmed often and sounded defeated whenever she'd ask me to do something. As if she had asked the boys to clean their room, you could practically hear me saying, "Mommy, do I have to?"

You know what the amazing thing is? Once I figured this out and dealt with my stuff, we had the best sex of our marriage. My wife didn't change anything, yet I got the intimacy I was craving and more than I had ever imagined possible. As for emotional load? I welcome it. I embrace it. I ask for more because I'm not burdened by the lies I told myself for years.

If something is keeping you from sharing mental load and some of the household tasks, figure out what it is. Do the work with a counselor, even if it's hard. It's not just your marriage that is suffering. You will always secretly feel inadequate or suffer from imposter syndrome if you don't address what's holding you back from shouldering your part of managing the home. But if you can embrace your responsibilities, the positive effects will likely spread to the bedroom!

Sometimes it's not you but your wife who doesn't take responsibility around the house or with the family. Or maybe she takes on so much responsibility that she won't give up any control to you or attempts to micromanage the tasks you are responsible for. Sit down and talk with her about how you both want the household to be organized. And, if necessary, have that conversation with a licensed counselor.

What If Your Wife Can't Turn Off "Mommy" Mode?

For some of you, it's not the housework that gets between you, it's the kids—sometimes literally. Nothing kills the mood more than kids piling into bed with you. Both the American Academy of Pediatrics and the Canadian Pediatric Society recommend room sharing but not bed sharing for infants.[3] But from talking to parents in my office, I know many still opt for cosleeping, which means sleeping with the babies in bed (often called the "family bed" in parenting literature). Moms often tell me they get more sleep that way, and they feel it builds intimacy and bonding.

I usually have the distinct impression that this is primarily the wife's choice and not the husband's. He may be going along with it because she insisted on it, but that doesn't mean he's happy about it. One husband wrote to Sheila, "Ever since our two-year-old was born, my wife has been sleeping with him. She claims, 'It is so much easier to breastfeed him when I am next to him.' This has been going on for twenty-eight months. She now sleeps in the same room with our toddler and our baby. We have not slept in the same bed for well over two years."

Now, if your wife is sleeping in another room with the children instead of with you, your marriage may be facing more serious issues than just sleep, and those issues should be addressed, ideally with a licensed counselor. But often families drift into cosleeping when babies are small and set up habits that are hard to break later for both Mom and child.

Certainly when you have small children, sleep is a serious issue. And if Mama's too tired, there's no action happening anyway. But think twice before you make it a habit to invite older babies and toddlers to share your bed perpetually. You need a place where you and your wife can be "just the two of you." Having kids there will kill your sex life. One cosleeping proponent once told Sheila that you could still keep your sex life alive, no problem: simply have silent, almost motionless sex! Personally, we can't imagine that being an ad for sex: *"Don't worry, honey, for the next few years we'll just have silent, motionless sex!"*

It's okay to say, "I love our kids and want to be the best dad I can be, but I also want to keep our bed just for us." Then take the lead on helping your child "be a big boy or girl" and adjust to sleeping in their own bed. It will be a difficult few nights and might be emotionally difficult for Mom. Maybe suggest she go out with friends or to a coffee shop on those evenings, and you be the one to help the kids adjust. Take on their bedtime routine. Be there if the kids wake up in the middle of the night and want to come back into bed. Don't simply tell your wife it is unacceptable; take responsibility for fixing it, and comfort everyone if the transition is emotionally difficult.

When Kids Grow

But children's interference in your sex life doesn't end when babies are out of your bed. Even when they grow, kids can put a damper on it. When you're afraid that kids will walk in or, perhaps worse, that they'll *know what you're doing*, sex can be seriously hampered.

One couple wrote to Sheila about how the vent for the heating ducts in their room was connected to the one in their teenagers' room. It was easy to hear what was going on in both rooms, which made it so hard for the mom to relax enough to have sex.

Listen to another woman who had an epiphany on a vacation: "On a recent trip, we had a hotel room all to ourselves where we didn't have to worry about waking up kids across the hallway. Whoa. I didn't even realize what had been missing. The mental energy involved in keeping things quiet had really prevented me from fully letting go!"

If your wife has difficulty relaxing because of the kids, reassure her that kids benefit from knowing that you both are still attracted to each other. Great parents gross out their kids! Certainly don't advertise what you're doing, but if teens hear the occasional bed squeak, that's better for them than to think you never make love at all. And white noise machines can cover up a multitude of sounds.

When we picture super sexy escapades, we often picture vacations—a hut in Fiji, a hotel room, a Caribbean resort. Why is that? Because it's away from our daily routines, where kids and housework and dinner prep and work inevitably get in the way. And those vacations are wonderful. If you get a chance to take them, do!

But you can't wait for vacations to nurture sex in marriage. If your relationship is going to be strong, sex has to be good even in the middle of the chaos. Yes, life is tiring. Yes, you have tons of competing demands on your time. Yes, kids are exhausting. But your relationship can be the anchor that helps give you energy to handle all those other parts of your life. So grow your friendship. Shoulder your share of the load. And be thankful that, even in the chaos, you're in this together.

CHAPTER 10

Let's Get Romantic

Greeting card companies try to convince you that romance means giving the perfect card. Chocolatiers try to convince you that romance is a box of chocolates. Others tell you it's diamonds or roses or a date night out, depending on who paid for the commercial.

Let's make this simple: romance is noticing what someone likes, then going out of your way to show them you were thinking of them and that you want them to be happy.

Being romantic with your wife might be buying chocolates or a card—if she happens to like that. It might be celebrating a date night with a chick flick. But it also might be picking up her favorite coffee drink or kissing her on the nose when she wakes up after you let her sleep in one morning. Romance doesn't have to be a big production. It can be those everyday little gestures that say *I notice. I care. I want to make you happy.*

Too often we say that women need romance, while guys need sex, but that's too simplistic. What guy doesn't also want to be noticed, to be cared for, to be happy? Romance is pursuing your spouse and intentionally living out your vows.

That's something we may do in an extra special way on Valentine's Day or on an anniversary, but that doesn't mean we're off the hook the rest of the year. No, a romantic marriage is one where you care for each other and pursue each other year-round.

Take the initiative to show your wife she's loved in whatever way works best for both of you.

For the tenth anniversary of our first date, I sent Sheila on a scavenger hunt all over our small town. In the card I left her that morning before I went to work, I told her to ask for a package at our local pharmacy at exactly 4:30 p.m. When there, she was handed a box of her favorite chocolate truffles, with a note to head to the jewelry store in the mall. There a pair of earrings was waiting for her, with another note sending her to a lingerie store. Finally she had a note directing her where to go for dinner, where she found me, in a suit, smiling at her as she walked in.

I put plenty of thought into it and earned major romance points, but the whole thing would have been much better if our credit card company hadn't interfered. In those days we didn't use our credit card very much; we mostly used cash. When our bank noticed all these transactions, they phoned Sheila to make sure she approved. They listed off all the stores I had gone to, spoiling my surprise! But she did a stellar job of looking amazed anyway.

Occasional grand gestures like that are important—and even mishaps like credit card companies can make them more memorable. But what we've found is that it's the daily romantic gestures that often count the most! When Sheila asked her female readers what romantic gestures they most appreciate, here's what came up most frequently:

- He reaches over and touches me when he's falling asleep.
- He makes me my coffee or tea in the morning—and brings it to me! (And one woman said that her husband ground the coffee beans in the garage so as not to wake her up.)
- He calls me at random times in the day just to hear my voice or to tell me he loves me.
- He kisses me goodbye before he leaves for work—or leaves for anywhere!

- He tells me I'm beautiful.
- He leaves little notes telling me he loves me.
- He charges my phone for me.
- He makes sure I'm drinking water and I'm hydrated.
- He puts gas in my car.

One woman wrote that their anniversary was 10/13—so every day at 10:13 a.m. and 10:13 p.m. her husband sends her a text telling her he loves her. In ten years he's only missed a few days—and even the kids get into it now!

These things are all tiny things, but tiny things that your wife appreciates, repeated regularly over time, show her that you value her. They can even be the mundane things, like "he fills up my CPAP machine every night," or "he started emptying the cat litter when I got pregnant six years ago, and he's never stopped," or "he starts the car for me in the winter and cleans off the ice." That's still romance—even if it would never be pictured on the front of a card.

Pursuing Your Spouse

Our wives don't just want to be seen and noticed, though; they also want to be wanted. Romance turned up a notch is pursuing her, wooing her, saying, "I want you."

But once you turn from "I love you" to "I want you," the dynamic shifts. You've stepped onto the ledge of vulnerability. You're putting yourself out there, knowing that you could be rejected, scoffed at, or ignored. Now, we hope those responses aren't common in your relationship, but surprisingly, it's that vulnerability that keeps a relationship fresh and close.

In a healthy marriage, both people will practice the art of romance. Both will care for the other. Both will take the initiative to help the other feel loved and wanted. If romance becomes lopsided, one of you will likely feel rejected, and one of you will bear the burden of the responsibility for keeping the marriage fresh. That tends to backfire.

If You've Left the Burden to Her

If you proposition your wife and are rejected, it hurts. If that happens frequently, it can be awfully tempting to give up on initiating anything. Being constantly rejected is a genuine problem, and if this has been your story, we urge you to seek out a licensed counselor and get to the bottom of why she doesn't want sex.

But sometimes it's fear of rejection that stops us men from pursuing our wives the way they need us to. Sometimes we dress it up with words that seem loving, like, "I don't want to pressure her!" Consider, though, that you may be putting all the work—all the vulnerability—on her. She shouldn't always have to be the one to pursue you because you're afraid of rejection.

Many women write to Sheila for help because their husbands never woo them but expect them to initiate sex anyway. A woman in this situation carries all the emotional load of getting in the mood, setting the stage for sex, and starting foreplay. And if she's one of those women for whom desire kicks in after excitement, it puts all the responsibility on her to "talk herself into it." Clearly this should not be the case. If you want your wife to be enthusiastic about sex, start by showing her you are enthusiastic about her, and that means being vulnerable enough to risk being turned down when you pursue her.

Then there are higher-drive wives who do most of the pursuing simply because they want sex more than their husbands do. Higher-drive wives bear a special burden because our culture often makes them feel they are abnormal, a message you should be careful not to feed. Now, certainly there's nothing wrong with you having the lower libido. But if your wife has a higher libido than you do, please understand that she doesn't only need sex from you—she also needs to feel like she's desirable, she's wanted, she's special. If you rarely initiate sex, she may start to wonder if she is undesirable. Don't leave her hanging. Part of marriage is showing your wife you want her. And as we discussed with the sexual response cycle, if you're someone for whom desire often kicks in after excitement, you can still get there by making the mental decision and jumping in with both feet. Neither spouse should have to initiate even 80 percent of the time. Everyone needs to feel desired. So show your wife you desire her. Even if you don't feel overwhelmed with desire beforehand, once you start touching and kissing and thinking about sex, your body will usually kick in.

HOW LOWER-LIBIDO HUSBANDS CAN MAKE THEIR WIVES FEEL DESIRED

- Build your friendship, and go to deeper levels of communication with her.
- Ask her about other ways you could make her feel attractive, and put those suggestions into practice.
- Read Sheila's book *31 Days to Great Sex* together as a couple.
- If you enjoy sex but have a more responsive libido, encourage her to initiate—and make an effort to respond when she does!
- Set realistic goals for yourself about initiating sex, and keep track of whether you are meeting them.

ADDRESSING CAUSES OF LOWER LIBIDO

Sometimes you may naturally fall on the lower end of the libido spectrum, and that's fine. But sometimes there are other reasons for lower libido that can and should be dealt with:

- Address any issues in the relationship, with a licensed counselor if necessary.
- Talk with a counselor about any trauma or baggage in your past.
- See a physician to check for low testosterone levels, medication side effects, or other medical conditions.
- Avoid pornography and masturbation.
- If stress from work or other aspects of life has caused your libido to tank, make some life changes to prioritize your relationship.
- If you have insecurities about sexual performance, be honest with your wife and try working through a challenge like those in *31 Days to Great Sex*.

If She's Left the Burden to You

What if you're the one who initiates the majority of the time and you're left wondering if she really wants you? Make sure you're doing everything else in this section to build your emotional connection and that she feels close to you. And then talk to her about it. Tell her it's important that you feel pursued too.

One answer might be that you need to pull back a bit. It could be that you've never given her libido time to kick in. Think of a balance scale. You may have reached a frustrating equilibrium where you are always the initiator and she is always the responder. If you want to change the equilibrium, you have two choices: you can wait for her to change up the balance, or you can change up the balance by backing off a little. If you do, you may find that when you step back, she discovers her sex drive again.

As far as practical tips, Sheila gave some in her book *31 Days to Great Sex*, in a section called "10 Ways Husbands Can Help Wives Get in the Mood":[1]

Unlike most men, women, on the whole, aren't usually "raring to go." We need to warm up to the idea of sex. That may seem odd because most women do enjoy sex, so why wouldn't we want to do it all the time? But if we're not specifically thinking about it and in the mood, then the idea of sex seems almost off-putting. A switch needs to be flipped so that we move from "turned off" to "turned on." For most (though not all) guys, that switch is almost always on; for women, it's not. Here's the hard thing about that switch: *guys can't flip it for us.* We need to turn it on ourselves.

We need to decide: "Okay, I want to feel sexy now."

A husband's job is simply to warm up a woman so that she is more likely to want to flip that switch. If he acts as if the switch is already flipped by making obvious sexual comments or by grabbing parts of her body as she walks by, chances are that she won't react well. But warm her up first so that she flips that switch, and then those advances are absolutely okay!

One woman explained this brilliantly on my Facebook page: "Don't act sexy! After a long day I don't want to feel propositioned. I want to feel like he's my best friend, like he still enjoys my conversation—laughing with me, etc. I want to know he thinks about and considers me!"

Here's the general progression:

WARMING UP ▶ FLIRTY ▶ SEXUAL

Once a wife is obviously flirting, then ramping it up is fine. But if she's still at the warming up stage, don't go straight to the sexual!

After that preamble, I (Sheila) gave ten hints for how to flirt, boost her libido, and even initiate sex. The first one we've already gone over in the last chapter: take on your share of the mental load and help around the house. The second is just as important in setting the scene: ask her how she's feeling or about her day or what's on her mind. Sometimes women have so many thoughts running through their heads that they need help processing them so they can make room for more sexy ones. Or if your wife is an internal processor, give her time to take a bubble bath so she can think. Once her concerns are taken care of, start flirting! Compliment her, offer to give her a massage, reminisce about a great memory together—anything that feels affectionate.

And then, once she's more relaxed, be more deliberate. Whisper what you've been dreaming about doing to her all day. Offer to take her out of her uncomfortable clothes. Or even throw this one in: "We tried something last time that you really liked, but I can't remember what it was. Can you remind me?" As with everything in your sex life, think of it as a progression. Warm her up before you get sexy. For some women, that's a long process. For others, it's much shorter. As you learn more about each other, chances are that the process will get shorter too. Honor her timing. Work with her body. And you'll both feel more satisfied.

Now that we've mastered making her toes curl in the bedroom, and making her feel secure and loved outside of it as well, let's turn to the last element of great sex: feeling completely and totally intimate with one another.

SPIRITUAL
INTIMACY
AND
ONENESS

CHAPTER 11

Making Love, Not Just Having Sex

On September 4, 1996, the phone rang at 1:30 in the morning. I (Sheila) was out of bed like a rocket because I knew what that meant. Earlier that evening we had said good night to our baby boy, lying in the pediatric intensive care unit at the Hospital for Sick Children in Toronto. Four days had elapsed since his open-heart surgery, and that day had not been a good one. But by the time we had left his bedside on September 3, he appeared to have turned the corner, and the danger seemed to have passed.

As soon as that phone rang, I knew that our relief was to be short-lived. The nurse on the other end of the line told me we had better come fast.

An hour later that same nurse brought out the body of our son and laid him in my arms.

We left the hospital at 3:30 a.m. and trudged the few blocks home. We climbed back into bed and didn't know what to do. We couldn't plan the funeral yet; it was the middle of the night. We couldn't go back to sleep. We were in shock. And so we held each other and kissed each other until the kissing turned into something more.

It was not that we were physically aroused. Rather, we were so

121

grieved and needed to be close to the only other individual on this earth who shared our pain. We needed to touch each other.

We hope you never have the need to make love in a moment of overwhelming grief, but at the same time, it was a precious experience for us because we both felt how sex was something so much deeper than physical pleasure. It was the joining of everything we were, the compulsive need to be united. A marriage is not complete if the couple has sex only for physical release; you also need that extraordinary spiritual closeness that was designed to come through sex.

Sex Is More Than Physical

In this book we describe the three aspects that go into great sex: learning how everything works physically, creating a great friendship that fuels your passion, and experiencing deep connection while you make love. It's that deep connection that we're going to turn to now. But that deep connection is often the hardest because it's the most fragile. It depends on being able to both express and feel love through sex.

Great sex is about making love, not just having sex. In great sex we become vulnerable and passionate, sharing the very essence of who we are. Great sex, then, isn't about saying, "I want sex." Great sex is about saying, "I want *you*." I want to know you. I want to experience everything with you. I want to feel like we are one. "Being one"—that spiritual connection—is the completion of physical intimacy and emotional intimacy. Once we figure out how our bodies work together, once we become vulnerable with one another and share with each other, then passion naturally flows.

Not surprisingly, in our survey, women who felt emotionally close to their husbands were more than five times more likely to reach orgasm. Feeling close, feeling *intimate*, fuels our physical response. You can't have real passion when it's just physical; connection to the other person is the real aphrodisiac.

Lucy Fry wrote for The Gottman Institute, the world's premier research institute on marriage, about what intimacy really means: "It is the place where emotional vulnerability and sexual desire collide and it is something we co-create; we cannot own it for ourselves."[1] Intimacy takes two; you can't force it. She goes on to say, "sexual intimacy can enhance emotional intimacy but without emotional intimacy, the sexual connection will reach its limits."[2]

We've talked about fueling that emotional connection already. But how, practically, do we bring it into the bedroom? Commenter Becky explained how her husband fostered intimacy:

Early in our marriage we were at a marriage conference where the speaker said that orgasm was a lot like imprinting. You know how little baby geese follow around whoever they see as soon as they are born? What they see first when they're born gets imprinted. And it's the same with us and orgasm. What we hear gets imprinted.

So my husband decided (without telling me) that every time he orgasmed, and every time I orgasmed, he was going to say, "I love you, Becky." He wanted those words to become the erotic ones in our marriage. So no matter how hot the sex is, even if we're being rather raunchy, he always says, "I love you, Becky," at that exact moment. He uses my name. And now sometimes he just leans over during the day and whispers it in my ear, and it definitely gives me warm fuzzies!

It's such a simple thing: saying I love you when you make love. But it helps us focus on why we're making love. Andrew Bauman, clinical counselor and author of *The Sexually Healthy Man*, explains some other ways to feel that deep connection during sex:

Start with five minutes of uninterrupted eye contact. Sit a foot apart from your spouse, and look into each other's eyes. No words, just lock eyes and hold the other's gaze. After the five minutes are up, talk about the experience. What did you see? How do you feel? After emotional connection is established, you can begin to explore connecting sexually.

Explore each other's bodies, communicating what brings each of you pleasure and what does not. Will you go slowly, practicing simply being with each other? Can you lay hands on each other's bodies and pray for each other? Will you learn the stories of each other's bodies? Each body part has a story to tell. Will you learn the stories of each body part and pray against Evil's accusations? Will you hold each other closely while naked? Will you and your partner hold eye contact while having intercourse?[3]

Some of his questions may leave you a bit hesitant. *Pray naked?* That sounds almost bizarre, doesn't it? We're used to thinking of God on one end of the spectrum and sex on the other, and never the two shall meet. But prayer can lead you into greater intimacy— which then fuels that urge to join together, to consume each other, to truly unite with each other. In prayer, we're vulnerable and honest before the One who made us. When our girls were younger, Sheila always told me the sexiest thing I could do was to pray out loud for our daughters. When she heard me praying for them at bedtime, she always said she wanted to jump me. (And when I got back to our room, quite often she did!) Our daughters were always so close to Sheila's heart and mind. When she heard me sharing my heart for the ones who so moved hers, it connected us.

Imagine the power, then, of praying over each other's bodies. Pray for the stretchmarks she still feels self-conscious about or the scar on your thigh from a bike injury you still have flashbacks about. Bless each other's bodies. Appreciate your bodies for all that they allow you to do for others and for each other. Imagine the freedom from shame that comes when your wife speaks blessings over the parts of you that you try to keep covered—in every sense of the word.

Prayer really can be hot! *Hot* and *holy* are not two words that generally go together, but when it comes to feelings of closeness and even to our sexual responsiveness, they should. Renaissance poets expressed this quite well. I love poetry because great poetry is more than just words; it speaks to us at the deepest level of emotion. Listen to what Shakespeare's contemporary, John Donne, wrote to God in his sonnet "Batter My Heart":

> Batter my heart, three-person'd God, for you
> As yet but knock, breathe, shine, and seek to mend;
> That I may rise and stand, o'erthrow me, and bend
> Your force, to break, blow, burn, and make me new.
> ....
> Take me to you, imprison me, for I,
> Except you enthrall me, never shall be free,
> Nor ever chaste, except you ravish me.[4]

He's asking God to overthrow him, to bend him, to break him, to conquer him. He's saying, I'll never be chaste unless you ravish me. Does that sound like a nice little orderly relationship where no one ever loses control? No, it's a tale of bending completely to another who overpowers you. That sounds a lot like passionate sex!

But John Donne wasn't some pervert. He was expressing the same thing that the Bible does when Paul writes in Galatians 2:20, "I have been crucified with Christ and I no longer live, but Christ lives in me. The life I now live in the body, I live by faith in the Son of God, who loved me and gave himself for me."

God lives in us, and we want more of him and less of us. As John the Baptist said of Jesus, "He must become greater; I must become less" (John 3:30). We yearn for God, and not only for his presence but for a deeply intimate relationship where we no longer feel alone but so imbued with him that we are finally complete.

The more we let ourselves be fully known and seen by God, despite our shame, despite our weaknesses, despite our failings, the more we will feel whole. And when that happens, it will cause us not to want to hide from our wives anymore either. We can let them in as well.

That brings us to another element of Andrew Bauman's intimacy-building suggestions: Will you and your wife maintain eye contact during intercourse? That turns vulnerability and intimacy up a notch, doesn't it? Eye contact when you're doing something so intensely personal lets another in. When vulnerability is scary, we're often quick to try to force a connection in a not-so-intimidating way. As men, especially, we have to avoid the temptation of equating orgasm with intimacy. When we're uncomfortable with emotions or with feeling seen, we will often yearn for the physical high from sex as an easier substitute. But doing that robs ourselves and our wives of our real need—to be truly seen and still be truly loved.

We may desperately hold back because that lets us keep control. It lets us keep a check on our emotions. But what if God made orgasm to teach us that staying in control is not the height of the human experience? In orgasm, we lose control. Clear thought is difficult, even speaking is difficult, and instead we speak in moans. We're not guarded, but rather we're carried along by the experience. There's a lesson there that God wants all of us to learn.

What do we think "self-control" means in the Bible? We usually think of someone who is always aware of their surroundings, who keeps their emotions in check and is calm and logical. We think that to be self-controlled means to be *in* control. But who is ultimately supposed to be in control of our lives? It certainly isn't us; it's God! That's what it means to walk in the Spirit—that God is in control. Maybe the point is not for us to be in control, but more about making sure we don't let *something other than God* be in control. To try to be in control by an act of our own will may sometimes be the opposite of what God wants.

And in orgasm God shows us that. For real intimacy, we have to give up control. We give up some bodily control as we turn ourselves over to passion and pleasure. To reach the height of passion, we also need to give up some emotional control and let her in—and share ourselves—too.

That connection is powerful. It's the urgency to consume her, to be consumed by her, so that you can feel even more connected. Intimacy is the gateway into great sex. And that requires being vulnerable, letting her see all of you, even the parts you don't like so much. As Andrew Bauman teaches, it's about living authentically and connecting with your wounds.[5] That sometimes means we have to dredge up ugly things that we want to keep hidden—the things that cause us shame, that make us want to run and hide, that we want to make sure no one sees.

But you can never have great sex when you haven't dealt with your shame or when you're still keeping secrets. She needs to see all of you; you need to see all of her. In this section, we're going to explore the most common areas we feel great shame about and try to keep hidden, and we're going to encourage you to look at them head-on so they stop having power over you and so they stop putting up roadblocks to the deep intimacy that God wants for you. It's going to be a heavy journey, but we hope that by the end of it, you'll feel more seen and heard. We hope you'll feel lighter. And we hope you'll see that sharing authentically and living in vulnerability with your wife is something you can do.

CHAPTER 12

When Sex Seems Ugly

One in four girls.

One in nine boys.[1]

The incidences of sexual assault and sexual abuse are horrendous.

God made sex to be an intimate knowing of two people. But when sex is turned into abuse—when it becomes a taking—then it's a deliberate *unknowing* of another human being. It says, "It's not just that I don't care about you. It's that you fundamentally don't matter, and I have the right to use you however I want." It's a rejection of the highest order. Not surprisingly, this causes real trauma, which impacts our physical bodies and our sexual lives.

In his groundbreaking book *The Body Keeps the Score*, Dr. Van der Kolk explains trauma this way: "Whenever we feel threatened, we instinctively turn to the first level, social engagement. We call out for help, support, and comfort from the people around us. But if no one comes to our aid, or we're in immediate danger, the organism reverts to a more primitive way to survive: fight or flight. We fight off our attacker, or we run to a safe place. However, if this fails—we can't get away, we're held down or trapped—the organism tries to preserve itself by shutting down and expending as little energy as possible. We are then in a state of freeze or collapse."[2]

Many of us have our sex lives permanently on that freeze mode because we've never been able to resolve trauma from our past. The parts of our brains that are activated during trauma stay activated, even when the danger has passed. And this can have dire consequences for our daily lives and our marriages, especially in the bedroom. Van der Kolk shows in the book the two forms of reactions to trauma—people in extreme agitation and emotional arousal (not sexual arousal, but having one's panic buttons constantly pushed) or people who are shut down, unable to feel emotions, connections, or experiences: "in an effort to shut off terrifying sensations, they also deadened their capacity to feel fully alive."[3] Thankfully, many trauma-informed licensed counselors now know how to help people recover from such trauma and live full lives again.

But trauma experts know that part of recovery is rediscovering a sense of agency over our own bodies. If you or your wife is a survivor of abuse, you must leave room for catering to the survivor's needs so healing can occur. For instance, survivors often find it easier to embrace their sexuality when they feel in control. Give the sexual assault survivor the freedom to stop in the middle of an encounter and say, "That's enough for tonight." If she's the survivor, positions where she is on top and she is the one doing the moving while you lie still may make her more comfortable. Or allowing her to explore your body during foreplay rather than you touching her may help her feel empowered and safe.

Then there are the triggers that can send the survivor back into panic mode. For Theresa, it was when her husband walked up behind her and put his arms around her waist. He was trying to show affection, but being touched when she didn't know it was coming made her heart rate race as her arms flailed. For James, it was being in the dark and hearing his wife's excited breathing. He found it much easier to make love with the lights on. It might be feelings, sounds, words, smells, even certain times of day, but something reminds the survivor of the abuse, and panic ensues and desire flees.

Triggers are not conscious or deliberate. If you or your wife has one, that is not a rejection of the other person. It is a trauma reaction that sends the survivor back to fight, flight, or freeze mode. With time, counseling, and increased trust, triggers can lessen in intensity. But in the meantime, learn to identify the triggers, honor them as much as possible, and don't take them personally.

When sexual abuse has been focused on a particular sexual act, maybe that act is simply off limits in the bedroom for the foreseeable future. Abuse leaves wounds, and a loving relationship will honor those wounds and allow them to heal rather than reopening them. As her husband, you may be the best source of healing that God has for your wife. And if you allow her to be, she may be a source of healing for you too.

Rachael Denhollander was cast into the spotlight when she became the first victim to go public in the Larry Nassar sexual assault trial. Nassar had victimized hundreds of women and girls in his role as a sports therapy physician. Rachael told Sheila in an email, talking about her marriage, "Working through the abuse together can be a long road, but it is a beautiful, redemptive road. Eventually, associations will be re-shaped into positive memories and experiences and a safe, secure, tender spouse can bring a depth of healing that seems beyond possible."[4] We hope that if sexual assault is a part of your story, you both will choose to walk that beautiful, redemptive road together.

Sometimes, though, it's not someone else who steals intimacy from us. It's the way we learn to talk about sex and think about sex, and we'll turn to that now.

When We Make Sex Sound Ugly

Think about some of the messages we often hear about sex, especially in evangelical circles. "Men are visually stimulated and easily tempted." "Have sex with him every seventy-two hours to make sure he doesn't stray or get tempted to lust." The way we often portray men's sex drives and talk about lust turns sex into something quite ugly, especially for women. They're the signs on the top of that mountain that are pointing us toward the thorny cactus instead of that lush garden.

We can't get to great sex using a route that steals honor and dignity from women while ascribing horrible motives to men. Unfortunately, that's what has been happening in the wider evangelical culture. It has hurt the guys who want to honor their wives, while killing the sex drives of their wives.

> We can't get to great sex using a route that steals honor and dignity from women while ascribing horrible motives to men.

In the last twenty years, sexuality has become a much bigger subject in churches, largely because it's become such a huge topic in the wider culture, and the church has had to respond. Pastors constantly talk to men who aren't getting enough sex. These pastors ask themselves, "How can we solve this sex-starved marriage problem?" They think maybe if women understood how their husbands were feeling and that sex should not be an optional part of marriage, then women would have more sex!

At the same time, the church has been rightly concerned about the plague of pornography. We've started preaching against porn and lust, warning everybody what a huge problem it is—it's "every man's battle." We tell teenage girls and women that they need to make it easier on men by what they wear. Then to wives we say, "You need to have sex more so he won't lust."

Now wives will start having sex, right? Because now they understand men's experiences. So things will be better, right?

Except they aren't.

Because this approach has exacerbated the problem.

To help you understand why, we want to ask you—just for a moment—to try to think about it from a woman's perspective. To start, let us ask this: Do you have a rape prevention strategy?

Every woman does. From as young as twelve years old or so, she can tell you all the assessments that constantly go through her mind, whether she's in a subway, walking on a road at night, or in a grocery store parking lot walking to her car. She is always aware of what's going on around her. She checks the back seat of a car before she gets in. She sits near the bus driver on the bus. If she feels nervous while walking at night, she gets on the phone with a friend and tells her exactly where she is so the friend can call 9-1-1 if necessary. Sexual violence is always in the background of her life.

Let's picture a young teenage girl who is forming her rape prevention strategies. She simultaneously has to accept living in a wider culture that objectifies her. In the grocery store, magazines blast pictures of women's breasts, and she knows she'll never measure up. She develops body image issues that never entirely go away. And she knows that men look. A lot.

This girl goes to youth group, where she and her friends are separated from the boys for "purity talks." She is told that boys will lust after her, and so when they go to pool parties, she needs to wear a T-shirt to stop all the boys from stumbling. She's told that she has to watch what she wears in church because she can cause her brothers in Christ to sin—and not only her fellow teens but adult men too. That presumably includes even the pastor and the elders.

In college she serves on the praise team. She is told to watch what she wears so that men in the front rows aren't able to look up her skirt and never to let cleavage show, or else men won't be able to worship. She wonders whether she wants to be on the praise team after all.

Most of her life she has to work not to see all men in a negative light. But eventually she falls in love and marries a great guy she thinks is honorable. But for whatever reason, they struggle with having passionate, fulfilling sex, and it happens less frequently than either of them would like.

When she goes to women's Bible study, she hears from marriage books that if she doesn't have sex, her husband will lust after other women. She is told that God created her to fulfill her husband's sexual needs, and if she doesn't meet them, he will look elsewhere, or at least be really, really, really tempted to.

Let me ask you honestly, men: If you were her, would those messages make you *more* likely to want to have sex or *less* likely to want it? Would they send the snowball down the hill toward great sex or toward the desert?

She has spent her whole life with the constant background noise of worries about sexual violence and being objectified. And then to be told that God says she needs to let her husband use her or he will fall into sin? It feels as if God is objectifying her too. It feels as if God is coercing her into sex. It feels as if no one cares that this is *her body*. She's been told again and again that her body belongs to her husband, not to her. Is this the message we want our wives to hear? Even if we ignore how unbalanced it is, we must see that by spreading it, we shoot ourselves in the foot.

Tragically, some in the church have come to see sex with the same viewpoint as the world: framing sex as solely physical. Pornography and the hook-up culture portray sex as only about pleasure and not about commitment. And when the church gives the message that sex is not about intimacy but entirely about ensuring that a husband has his physical needs met, it makes the very same error.

Yes, you have physical urges toward sex, and those drives are good, and they are from God. But those urges aren't the whole story. To have a great, healthy sex life, we need to tell God's whole story. A route down the right side of the mountain calls us to something with greater dignity, something better than meeting just physical needs. It points to a God who loves us, a God who doesn't want anyone to feel guilty or used. It points to mutually satisfying sex that is for both of us, not sex that was created primarily for one person or prioritizes one of you over the other.

Too many of the messages about sex from Christian resources leave women feeling that sex is dirty, gross, or demeaning and reduce women's ability to enjoy it. Take, for example, the obligation sex message. If a woman believes she is obligated to give her husband sex when he wants it, she is 24 percent less likely to be satisfied with the amount of foreplay in their marriage and 29 percent more likely to infrequently orgasm.

And what about when guys believe these messages? They're 119.7 percent less likely to make her pleasure a priority, and their wives are almost 31.3 percent less likely to orgasm reliably. And that's not all!

How does a husband believing that his wife is obligated to give him sex when he wants it affect the couple's marital and sexual satisfaction? (What percent more or less likely are they to experience the following?)	
I reliably orgasm during sex	-119.7%
I make my wife's sexual pleasure a priority	-115.3%
My wife reliably orgasms during sex	-31.3%
My wife feels comfortable bringing up her sexual desires and preferences with me	-27.6%
My wife is satisfied with how frequently she orgasms during sex	-25.9%
When we argue, I don't feel my wife really hears me	86.1

If we're going to send the snowball down the right side of the mountain, we need to let these unhealthy messages about sex fall by the wayside and replace them with good ones. Intimacy is always the aim; oneness is always the goal. Sex should always be something that grows intimacy, not something that detracts from it. We want you to keep looking into each other's eyes because sex is something you do together, not turning away from truly seeing her because you want to prioritize yourself. Let's look at how to keep that healthy oneness approach at the center of our sexual expression in marriage.

CHAPTER 13

Is Sex a Need?

Sheila here! Before we got married, Keith and I were totally hot for each other. While kissing is all we really did, it was sometimes quite passionate, and neither of us wanted to stop. We counted down the days until the wedding night. I looked forward to what it would be like when we could finally make love. And I would think about it rather graphically too!

Then, about two months before our wedding, I was given one of the bestselling Christian sex books at the time, *The Act of Marriage* by Tim and Beverly LaHaye. It was over thirty years ago now, and at the time I couldn't put my finger on exactly what was so bad about it. But as I was reading it, I felt my whole body stiffen and grow cold. I tended to read books in the bathtub in those days, and by about two-thirds of the way into the book, I was so angry that I took that book and drowned it until it was dead. And then I unceremoniously dumped it in the garbage, which is where I wish I had put it in the first place.

The overwhelming feeling I got after reading that book was, *I don't have a choice anymore. He can use my body any time he wants.* Now, remember: I was someone who was looking forward to sex, more than anything I had ever looked forward to in my life. But when *The Act of Marriage* made me feel I had no right to say no, all of a sudden the very nature of sex changed for me. It wasn't something

I was doing because I wanted to; it wasn't me sharing myself with Keith. If I had to have sex when Keith wanted it, then what I felt no longer mattered. Then I no longer mattered. Sex, instead of being about *us*, became about *him*.

We were utterly dismayed when, on our wedding night, we couldn't even consummate our marriage because sex hurt too much. I had a full-blown case of vaginismus—when the vaginal muscles contract so much that penetration becomes painful or impossible.

Twenty-nine years later I was involved in the huge survey we've been telling you about, and one thing that survey revealed was that women going into marriage believing they are obligated to have sex have a 37 percent higher rate of vaginismus. I was a textbook case. Our study found that the obligation sex message has virtually the same statistical effect on women's rates of sexual pain as prior trauma, likely because they have something in common.[1] Both trauma and the obligation sex message say, "Your needs don't matter. Someone else has the right to use you." When we make sex about obligation, then it's no longer about a knowing. Rather, it becomes an owing. And that doesn't build intimacy, it destroys it.

> When we make sex about obligation, then it's no longer about a knowing. Rather, it becomes an owing. And that doesn't build intimacy, it destroys it.

So here's a young guy who really wants sex and a young woman who is looking forward to enjoying it too, and then everything gets messed up when it's no longer about doing what you want to do, but instead becomes about doing what you have to do. In our survey of women, this was the most damaging message that women had internalized: that she is obligated to have sex when he wants it and that she can't say no without being in sin. And in our survey of men, 23.4 percent believed it.

But the Bible *Does* Say "Do Not Deprive"

The obligation sex message comes from a misinterpretation of 1 Corinthians 7:3–5, which says:

> The husband should fulfill his marital duty to his wife, and likewise the wife to her husband. The wife does not have authority over her own body but yields it to her husband. In the same way, the husband does not have authority over his own body but yields it to his wife. Do not deprive each other except perhaps by mutual consent and for a time, so that you may devote yourselves to prayer. Then come together again so that Satan will not tempt you because of your lack of self-control.

Does "do not deprive each other" mean we are obligated to have intercourse whenever our spouse wants it? Here's how Sheila explained it in *The Great Sex Rescue*:

> When we say "Do not deprive," we're saying, "Someone has a need that has to be fulfilled." But this is not the same thing as saying, "A person gets to have whatever they want." God made us with a need for food. If your child asks, "Can I have Cheetos?" and you refuse because lunch is in an hour, you are not depriving her of food. The child's need is for a healthy, balanced diet, not to eat anything she wants, any time she wants.[2]

The whole point of the 1 Corinthians 7 passage is how *mutual* sex is. It's not about him getting his needs met but how both of their needs matter. If anything, her needs are mentioned first!

Sex is a necessary part of a healthy marriage, but a wedding license is not an IOU for sex. A wedding license is like a driver's license: getting a driver's license gives you permission to drive; it does not give you a car, much less pay for the gas. Likewise, a marriage license means that you are now in a relationship where sex is sanctioned. You are not, however, owed sex. Sex is the culmination of everything else in your relationship.

Now, since in marriage we commit ourselves to be sexually faithful to only one person, we certainly do need to hold our spouse's sexual desires and drives with care,

> Sex is a necessary part of a healthy marriage, but a wedding license is not an IOU for sex.

knowing that we're their only object of sexual attention. But no matter what, each of our other needs matters as well. God did not make sex so that one person's needs could erase the personhood of another.

When Sheila talked about the obligation sex message on her blog, a woman responded with this insight:

> I am nursing our fourth baby and am newly pregnant with our fifth. Typically I have had a very healthy libido, but this pregnancy, not so much. My body simply will not respond. Is it my job to give my husband sexual favors if I can't have intercourse? I know I am probably wrong here, but I went into marriage believing that sex was a mutual giving and receiving of love, not just a legal physical release. I know he has needs (and we have sex at worst twice a week, except during my cycle), and sometimes I would like to satisfy him when I can't fully participate, but the idea that it is my job, that I was created to be his sexual outlet without a choice; that sex, in his own words, is about using each

other for our own pleasure . . . Well, this creates pretty deep feelings of resentment, self-hatred, and loneliness.

If I do favor him, at his urging, I struggle that much more the next time we have reciprocal sex. If the sex desire I'm fulfilling has nothing to do with me or our love or a relationship and everything to do with just physical urges, then sex seems ugly. I don't say this from a selfish desire to achieve my own climax. I just strongly resent being a tool, and I know my husband believes my view is sinful. How do I change? How do I submit to being used, without resentment?

Think about her last question: *How do I submit to being used?* You will never achieve great sex if your wife feels like she is being used. When someone feels used, intimacy by any definition is impossible. Sex is meant to be a mirror of the deep longing for true connection that God has for us. It is not simply physical; it is also emotional and spiritual. That intimacy is life-affirming and life-giving. It says, *You are worth knowing. You are worth exploring. You are worth loving.* These should be your words to your wife, her lover's words.

> You will never achieve great sex if your wife feels like she is being used.

Look at that very word—*lover.* We call someone we have sex with our lover because we share something deeply personal and intimate. Reduce it to mere physical release and it is no longer two lovers in bed with each other, looking deeply into each other's eyes, praying blessing over one another. It is the relationship of a master and a servant. And there is no intimacy between a master and a servant.

If we're ever going to have great sex, we must abandon any sense of entitlement. In Sheila's focus groups for wives, women reported over and over that their desire for sex blossomed when their husbands finally gave them permission to say no to sex—or even to stop in the middle of intercourse when it wasn't working for them. When husbands reassured their wives that they could stop, well, suddenly they became orgasmic after never experiencing pleasure before. Everything finally clicked.

One of Sheila's frequent commenters is a woman who married recently for the first time, in her forties. She suffers from a variety of health conditions that lead to chronic pain. She started following Sheila's blog before the wedding so she could learn all she could about sex. She wrote,

> As an older, newly married couple, and with some health issues in the equation too, we went into marriage knowing that we were likely to have some physical limitations on how often we had sex. And we agreed from the start that either of us has total freedom to say if we just want to cuddle or go straight to sleep instead of doing something more "energetic"! We've only chosen the "straight to sleep" option about three nights in the last six months, and I think it's largely due to having the freedom to communicate what we want. So nights when we're both quite tired, we'll often say "let's see how far we get"—and surprise ourselves! I reckon the freedom to say, "Sorry, I'm suddenly really tired, can we sleep now?" without the other person taking it as rejection has been one of the most beneficial things in our sex life because it takes all the pressure away.

Exactly. When you have the freedom to say no, suddenly you also have the freedom to say an enthusiastic yes!

What about When Sex Is off the Table for a Time?

If sex is off the table for a time because of her health or her body's normal cycle, your primary consideration should not be your own needs, but hers. Let's talk about something that makes a lot of guys freak out: her period. Guys, can I be frank? If you were the one bleeding out of your genitals, would your first thought be how difficult it must be for your wife not to have access to them? Yet bestselling Christian books have framed a woman's period as a difficult time for her husband, talking about the importance of her giving him sexual favors during her period because he shouldn't be expected to go more than seventy-two hours without release.[3] We simply need to stop talking about her period and her postpartum phase and her chronic pain—or whatever it may be—as being a difficult time *for us.*

Most women experience at least some cramping during their periods, and many experience far more. Many have heavy bleeding and bloating. They feel extra sensitive, both physically and emotionally. Now, some women find their hormone levels make sex super fun during that time of the month, and 15 percent of women enjoy sex during their periods.[4] If she does—and you do—more power to you! But the vast majority of women find even the idea of sex during their periods distinctly unsexy.

And that applies doubly for the postpartum phase. Certainly intercourse will be off the table until the doctor gives the go-ahead (usually six weeks, but many women take longer than that to heal). But even if you consider other sexual activity, remember that your wife has just pushed a human out of her vaginal canal, or she's gone through major surgery to give life to your baby. She is getting little sleep. Her milk is either coming in and she's leaking all the time, or else she's stressed because the milk *isn't* coming. She has major hormone swings. She may have had a major tear during delivery and may have difficulty walking or need to take baths with salts to soothe the perineal area.

This is a difficult time *for her.*

Ephesians 5:28 says, "Husbands ought to love their wives as their own bodies. He who loves his wife loves himself." If she is bleeding, in pain, exhausted, uncomfortable, and dealing with hormone swings and you look at her and say, "But what about my orgasm?" then in what possible way are you loving her as your own body?

People often present sexual impulses as innately irresistible, but that is not the case. Let's remember that in Leviticus, God himself expected men to abstain every month for longer than a typical menstrual period.[5] And husbands in the Old Testament weren't even allowed to touch their wives during their periods. Women lived in a separate tent with other women. *God expected that men could last during her period.* And after the birth of a baby? The husband was required to wait either forty days or eighty days, depending on the sex of the child.[6] And this wasn't abstaining only from intercourse but from *any* sexual contact. We're certainly not under Old Testament law anymore, but it is worth pointing out that even under the old covenant, God did not feel this was unreasonable to ask of men. He did not think that after seventy-two hours without sex, guys would start sinning. God seemed to think that people back then could practice self-control and honor one another's bodies. Should we, who are indwelled by the Holy Spirit, do any less?

Some women will have a harder time physically with pregnancy and childbirth than others. Maybe your wife will feel perfectly fine during pregnancy, or maybe she will be so nauseated during the first trimester that all she can think about is what food she can possibly keep down. Either way, her body and her health matter because she is growing your child. Or postpartum, she may have no issues at all, or she may experience pain with intercourse, as do 26.7 percent of the women in Sheila's survey. Love her like you would love your own body. Recognize—and let her know that you recognize—that your sex life will obviously change during these times, rather than putting more pressure on her.

Loving each other and giving to each other is a great thing, but when that giving is entirely one way (she gives despite her physical discomfort, and he doesn't exercise self-control), then it is no longer about two lovers giving. It's about one person taking from another. That has no place in an intimate, Jesus-centered marriage. And for a man to tell his wife that God wants her to let herself be used for his enjoyment cuts to her very soul. It's not just that it makes her do something she gets no pleasure from; it also robs her of the beauty of sex that she was designed to experience.

And when you rob her, you end up robbing yourself too.

Until we treat women as objects of love rather than objects to be used, we will never experience the beauty of sex the way God intended. Rather, we will kill their spirits. And when a woman's spirit is killed, the ability to experience intimacy is wiped out because she's been told, "I don't honor you, so I don't honor what you have to share."

Besides, remember that most women enjoy the best sex a decade or two into marriage, not in the early years. If you feel like you're in a sexual desert during pregnancy or postpartum months, the best is yet to come. But it will arrive sooner if you don't let that snowball roll down the wrong side of the hill. And if you push for one-sided sex when it hurts her? That snowball will go faster and faster down the wrong side!

What Does Sexual Coercion Look Like?

Why are we getting so riled up about this? Well, when Sheila reviewed all the bestselling evangelical marriage and sex books for her book *The Great Sex Rescue*, she noticed that one critical word was missing from every single one of them (even though the bestselling secular resources handle the topic well): consent.[7] Far too many evangelical resources included stories of marital rape and didn't even specify that this was wrong.[8] When Sheila did her survey of twenty thousand women, many volunteered to be part of focus groups. Of those who volunteered, roughly one fifth wanted to tell us their stories of marital rape.

We can't write a book to men without explaining clearly that marital rape is sinful, evil, and illegal and that rape does not always involve physical force. Nonconsensual sex occurs any time a person feels they cannot say no. If they can't say no, then they can't truly say yes—they can't freely consent.

You can coerce your wife into sex in many ways:

- If you withhold money, give her the silent treatment, or are irritable or angry with her if you don't have sex, that's coercion.
- If you use a sex toy on her without her consent, have sex with her while she's sleeping, or do an act that she has already said she didn't want, that's rape and assault, even if she has an orgasm from that act.[9]
- If after you have sex with her you yell at her less, or yell at the children less, so she feels as if she has to have sex to manage your moods and keep others safe, that's coercion.
- If you use Bible verses as a weapon against her, that's coercion, and it's also spiritually abusive.
- If you tell her that the only way you can stop watching porn or lusting or having an affair is if she has sex with you, then that's coercion.

Yes, you may feel sexually frustrated, and we'll talk about that more at the end of the book. But sexual frustration does not give you license to coerce your wife into giving you an orgasm.

Pushing the Snowball Back Up the Hill

What if the obligation sex message has already messed up your marriage? If she's felt she had to have sex or else bad things would happen, then that has likely done some damage to her libido and sexual response. How do you restore a healthy view of sex?

Take a Sex Hiatus

Taking a sex hiatus can take different forms. Take sex entirely off the table for a period of time, like a few weeks or a month, to grow the relationship, have fun together, and show her that you can love her without sex. Alternatively, make sex entirely about her for the next little while. Don't worry about your orgasm. Rather, focus on her sexual pleasure instead of your own climax to show that you can live without release.

Give Her Permission to Stop at Any Point

Tell her that if sex stops feeling good for her, or if she suddenly changes her mind, you want her to speak up and even stop if need be! Show her that you want sex only if she's 100 percent there with you. That is often the key to awakening her libido.

Ask Her If She Feels Safe or Free to Stop

Does your wife feel panicky if you haven't had sex in a few days, as if you will feel unloved, grumpy, or resentful? Does that panicky feeling usually lead to duty sex rather than a genuine desire for sex? Does she feel free to stop if she doesn't like what's happening, or is she too afraid of disappointing or frustrating you?

Sometimes women internalize the obligation sex message, and you may never even realize it. This could be what is holding you back from great sex. Ask your wife if anything in this chapter resonates with her, and then listen to her. Together, you can make sex into a true experience of oneness.

CHAPTER 14

You Don't Need That Fix

Watching porn is bad.

Chances are you already know that, so we won't belabor it. What isn't talked about enough, though, are the effects of porn, including its most tragic one: it's one of the leading contributors to sex trafficking worldwide.[1] Porn depicts the real sexual abuse of women and children (and men). And porn hurts marriages too. Absolutely. Catching their husbands using porn is a deep betrayal for many women, and rebuilding trust and a healthy sex life can be an uphill battle.

But here's some good news: *Just because you used porn in the past does not mean your marriage is doomed.*

Keep using porn today, though? You'll create a world of hurt.

We'd like to do something tricky in this chapter. We'd like to have a nuanced conversation about porn, which involves both chucking out the myths around it but also fully accepting the facts about porn's effect on marriages—even if it makes us feel uncomfortable.

Myth #1: When I Get Married, the Temptation to Use Porn Will Decrease

Porn and sex are not the same thing. Sex is an intimate knowing of another person; porn is about using someone for your gratification. What makes porn exciting is that it's always new and different, but your wife can't be new and different. Many men get married thinking that sexual release through intercourse with their wife will dull the need for porn, but most find that it does not.

Myth #2: Men Watch Porn Because Their Wives Don't Have Enough Sex with Them

When we're talking about porn use in marriage, we have to realize that for the majority of porn users, the porn came before the marriage, not the marriage before the porn. For men under forty in our study, porn habits started before marriage 82.4 percent of the time (see following graph).[2] Even for men over forty, most still started before marriage. And we would suggest another reason why almost half of the rest of them started after marriage: it likely has less to do with the marriage itself than that these older men were already married when the online pornography explosion happened. Today's porn habits are far more associated with the accessibility of internet pornography than they are the willingness of wives to have sex.

And the younger a man is when porn habits develop, the more destructive they can be because porn often becomes the method

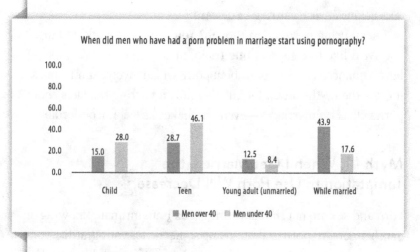

When did men who have had a porn problem in marriage start using pornography?

of choice for dealing with uncomfortable feelings. Are you bored? Frustrated? Feeling rejected? Porn seems to help because the hormonal rush at orgasm can soothe those negative emotions. We channel our brokenness and sadness and pain into pornography because it's safer than dealing with what's going on in our hearts. But when you make it a habit to turn to porn to deal with difficulties, then it's even more likely porn will beckon once you're married. The problem is not a lack of sex but rather a lack of other coping strategies and a fear of looking below the surface.

Myth #3: 80 Percent (Or Some Other Super High Number) of Christian Husbands Currently Use Porn

Our survey found that 73.4 percent of men report that porn has been an issue for them *at some point*. But only 6.5 percent of men were currently using porn on a regular basis. Yes, 16.7 percent have intermittent binges, and another 26.5 percent use it rarely, but half of the men we surveyed never use it at all today.

Myth #4: If a Guy Has Used Porn, It Has Permanently Rewired His Brain about Sex in a Way That He Can Never Fully Recover From

Porn certainly *does* rewire your brain, and it takes time (and much work, humility, and counseling) to recover, but it can be done. The majority of men have used porn at some point in their lives, yet most are still able to have healthy sex lives. Difficulties stem from *how much* porn you've watched, whether porn ever became a regular part of your life, and whether you're truly committed to stopping.

When porn use never becomes a regular habit, when it is fought against and rejected, then it's likely that the guy will still enjoy a healthy sex life with his wife without major counseling. And even for men whose porn use has become a regular and persistent habit and needs more work to overcome, remember that he who is in us is greater than he who is in the world (1 John 4:4). Jesus can help recovery from porn, even if that process is messy and difficult.

Those are the myths about porn use. Now let's look at the facts.

Fact #1: Porn Use Is a Betrayal of Your Wife, and She Will Likely Feel Upset and Even Traumatized by It

When you married, you vowed to "forsake all others," and if you use porn, you have broken that promise. Sex is supposed to be mutual, pleasurable, and intimate. It's supposed to be a deep "knowing" of each other. You have put that in jeopardy. You may honestly feel that your porn use has nothing to do with her and does not change how you feel about her, but none of that will make it any less painful for her.

When women discover their husbands' porn use, most feel betrayed, horrified, and even disgusted. Several studies now suggest that the majority of wives of sexually addicted spouses have trauma-related responses and need counseling themselves.[3] Even once you have worked to break the habit, she will likely need you to prove your fidelity before she'll be able to freely enter a sexual relationship again—and some women do feel the betrayal is too much to come back from. Other women push themselves to provide even more frequent sex, hoping this will keep you from porn. This dynamic can accentuate betrayal trauma since it is based in fear. Show her you are trustworthy outside the bedroom, and allow her to set the pace with rebuilding a sex life—or deciding whether she wants to rebuild at all.

Fact #2: You Will Make Everything Worse by Deflecting Responsibility onto Her

Some men, when caught in porn use, blame their wife's lack of sexual availability as the main issue—or at least as a contributing factor. A husband blaming the wife for his own sin literally goes back to the first few pages of the Bible, but it didn't fool God then, and it doesn't fool him (or anyone else!) now. Recovery from porn will be a difficult road, but you will make it much more challenging if you start that journey by blaming her.

Similarly, while she can support your recovery, you must never suggest or imply that your commitment to defeating this issue rests on her. Your repentance and recovery from porn relies on your leaning on Jesus (and counselors and support groups) for what you need, not your wife. First Corinthians 7 is not about a wife standing in the gap between her husband's lust problem and his porn addiction. If you struggle with an unhealthy relationship with sex, don't put that on her shoulders.

Tragically, too many Christian resources wrongly place the responsibility to help a guy kick porn on the wife. *Every Man's Battle*, for instance, said, "Your wife can be a methadone-like fix when your temperature is rising."[4] Think about what that implies: she needs to drug you so that you don't go after what you *really* want. She is merely a substitute for what entices you more. That is not sexy. That's not biblical. That's not right. And that's not what a loving husband wants in a marriage. Nevertheless, it is what 28.6 percent of the men in our survey believe—my wife should have sex with me to stop me from watching porn. And this has devastating effects on men's sex lives.

What happens when women believe they have to have sex to stop his porn addiction? They're 33 percent more likely to engage in sex with their husbands *only because they believe they have to*. If you want mutually fulfilling sex, you must guard against making her feel coerced in any way. Take responsibility for what you have done and for getting better.

If porn use has become a compulsive habit, then your porn problem likely is not even ultimately rooted in sex—no matter how much it may feel like it is. As Michael John Cusick, a

How does a husband believing that sex in marriage prevents porn use affect a couple's marital and sexual satisfaction? (How many times more or less likely are they to experience the following?)	
I feel that my wife considers my needs, desires, and wants in our marriage as much as she does her own	-2.1
When we have conflict, I feel my wife "hears me"	-2.0
I am satisfied with the amount of enthusiasm my wife shows in the bedroom	-2.0
I am satisfied with the amount of adventure my wife shows in the bedroom	-1.8
I make my wife's sexual pleasure a priority when we have sex	-1.7
I am comfortable bringing up difficult conversations with my wife	-1.7
My wife makes my sexual pleasure a priority when we have sex	-1.6
I am comfortable talking to my wife about what feels good sexually and what I want sexually	-1.5
I am satisfied with the amount of closeness I share with my wife during sex	-1.4
My wife frequently orgasms during sex	-1.3

counselor specializing in sexual addiction recovery, explains, porn supplies "validation of your manhood without requiring strength."[5] It makes you feel like a man even when you're broken, lonely, weak, or scared. Porn helps you *feel* strong without requiring you to *be* strong. So when you feel broken, when you feel wounded, porn helps you temporarily forget your feelings of inadequacy. But sex will never fix the wound, let alone porn. It will be healed only by allowing yourself to confront and feel your weakness and shame and open up those parts of you to God. As Cusick put it, "Addictions are strategies we use to keep the truth from ourselves by blinding us from seeing what's true about us."[6] Seeing our wounds is scary. It's easier to cover the deep thirsts we have for affection, validation, affirmation, respect, significance, security, or any number of good and necessary desires with porn or even sexual release from our wives. Both these things can make us feel strong. But it's a false strength, and eventually it won't be enough.

Fact #3: Most Men Who Use Porn Today Got Trapped When They Were Young

Porn habits are often cemented when guys are young. And if guys battle porn as children or preteens, it is often because someone else introduced them to it. Sometimes that someone was a friend, or sometimes relatives left porn lying around. And sometimes adults showed boys porn. In most jurisdictions, showing a minor pornography is illegal. Seeing porn as a minor can be traumatizing and can form a pull toward porn that is based on trauma.

Andy's dad left porn around the house when Andy was a kid, and it fascinated him. One night when he was ten, he grabbed a magazine and was masturbating in his room when he heard his parents fighting.

How does male porn use change across the lifespan? (What percent of male Christians have self-described problematic porn use at different life stages?)

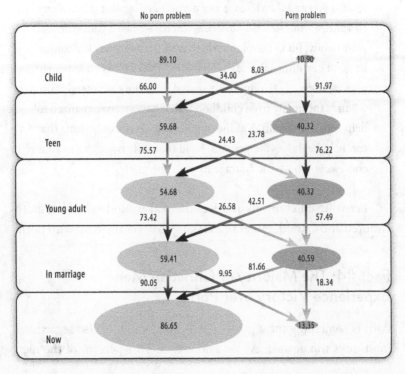

A few months later his parents divorced. He always felt that God had punished him for masturbating because the two seemed intertwined in his mind. He felt guilt and shame, but he also felt alone because his parents were not emotionally available to him. He started masturbating more and more. Today, twenty years later, he's in an unhappy marriage. He wants to quit porn, but every time he feels belittled by his wife, the shame returns, and he turns to pornography again.

Is Andy's porn use a sin? Certainly. But it's also tied up with feelings of shame and trauma, and what Andy needs is not only repentance but also healing of his childhood wounds that made him susceptible to a porn habit in the first place.

When Andrew Bauman counsels sex addicts who were introduced to porn as children, he encourages them to grieve:

> The loss of innocence, the betrayal of your body, the violence against you and the violence you perpetrated against others. Your cowardice, your lies, the suffering you have caused your wife and your family, fill in the blank, there is much to grieve. We cannot let go of our unhealthy sexual patterns until we have adequately grieved them. . . . Compulsive sexual behaviors are merely core wounds (normally from childhood) that have been sexualized to help soothe the pain. Kindness not cruelty is the only thing that can help heal the younger you. Hold that little boy close to your chest as you have the courage to welcome grief.[7]

Let yourself confront and feel the real wounds you have both endured and caused, rather than trying to cover them up with porn.

Fact #4: The Majority of Christian Men Experience Victory over Porn

Porn is something most guys fight against, and it is also something most guys *win* against. As we said earlier, 73.4 percent of the men we surveyed report that porn use had been frequent enough at some point in their life that they considered it a problem, but only 13.3 percent report that they have a porn problem now.[8] Yes, some men relapse, and sometimes intermittent porn use becomes a way of life. That's not okay, and if it keeps happening, seek professional help. But universally shaming men will only make the issue worse. We need to be voices of healing and hope and not write off our young men as monsters or as no longer being marriage material. Our concern should be less about whether porn has ever been in their lives in the past and more about helping Jesus be evident in their lives now.

Fact #5: Porn Has a Dose-Response Effect

Porn is a great example of what we call in medical circles a "dose-response effect." People respond based on the dose they've been given. The longer you've used porn, the more porn you've used, and the younger you started using porn, the greater these effects will be.

A clear example of this in our research is the effect of porn use frequency on the rate of erectile dysfunction: the more a man uses porn, the more likely he is to have erectile dysfunction. The biggest dose of porn (daily) has the largest effect. Men who use porn daily were just over twice as likely to have erectile dysfunction as men who never use it.

■ ■ ■

Steve began using porn when he was fourteen, when his friends started texting videos back and forth. Soon it became a nightly habit. When he left for college, he stopped for a time, but when exam season came around, he felt so stressed that he turned to porn to relieve pressure. A few years later, when he and Jackie married, he thought his porn use would diminish, and for a while it did. But Jackie wasn't that adventurous in bed, and he often found himself being pulled toward something more enticing. He'd lock himself in the bathroom at night and scroll on his phone, masturbating.

At first he found he could handle his marriage and the porn at the same time. He knew Jackie felt distant from him because he often preferred going into the bathroom than spending time with her at night, but she didn't complain that much. In fact, when the babies were small, he convinced himself he was doing her a favor since he wasn't bothering her for sex as much. But when their youngest was two, Jackie wanted to go away for the weekend for their anniversary. She asked him to leave his phone at home. He felt antsy, and for the first time in their marriage, that night he couldn't perform. The next morning, when they tried again, it took forever for him to climax, and he could tell she was annoyed with him. He felt like it would be easier if she did something other than just lie there. He found it way sexier to take her from behind, but she always complained that it didn't feel good and she didn't like it. He knew he'd have an easier time if she performed oral sex on him, but she kept wanting "regular" sex. That night his erection failed him too. He became worried because he was only thirty-four years old.

Back at home, he found that his penis still performed if he was in the bathroom with his hand and his phone. With his wife, though, he could no longer get it up. He stopped initiating sex, but Jackie started initiating more and more. She even bought racy leather lingerie that he knew made her uncomfortable. It had the desired effect on his erection the first time, but then it lost its magic. He was afraid that he'd lost sex forever.

■ ■ ■

Porn affects men's libidos, men's sexual function, even men's generosity in bed, all for the worse, because porn trains us to think of sex in selfish terms. In porn, women don't require foreplay. In fact, women aren't considered much at all. They're just used. And we see this in our stats of how men who use porn perform in bed too.

We found that men who use porn daily are 6.13 times less likely to frequently orgasm during sex with their wives than men who never do. More effects of porn on male sexual satisfaction are shown in this graph.

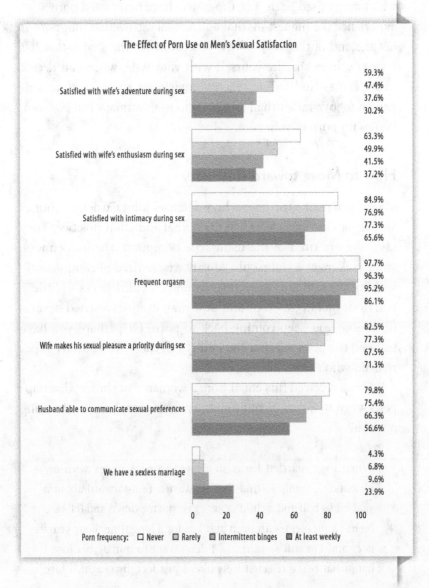

The Effect of Porn Use on Men's Sexual Satisfaction

Category	Never	Rarely	Intermittent binges	At least weekly
Satisfied with wife's adventure during sex	59.3%	47.4%	37.6%	30.2%
Satisfied with wife's enthusiasm during sex	63.3%	49.9%	41.5%	37.2%
Satisfied with intimacy during sex	84.9%	76.9%	77.3%	65.6%
Frequent orgasm	97.7%	96.3%	95.2%	86.1%
Wife makes his sexual pleasure a priority during sex	82.5%	77.3%	67.5%	71.3%
Husband able to communicate sexual preferences	79.8%	75.4%	66.3%	56.6%
We have a sexless marriage	4.3%	6.8%	9.6%	23.9%

Porn frequency: ☐ Never ☐ Rarely ☐ Intermittent binges ▨ At least weekly

Fact #6: Most Past Porn Users Recover

Thankfully, when men stop using porn, their rates of sexual and marital satisfaction improve so much they're almost equal to guys who haven't used porn. Yes, those who have never used porn at all experience the highest marital and sexual satisfaction. But porn is not the end of the story. When you deal with the shame that has kept you from sharing yourself with your wife, when you decide to see sex as God sees it, when you view your wife as a precious person to love rather than as a body to use, intimacy can blossom, even with porn in your past.

How to Move toward Recovery

Maybe you're like the guys whom Michael John Cusick, author of *Surfing for God*, has treated in his sexual addiction practice. They say, "We are tired of the using, the deception, the hiddenness, and the damage to our souls. Mostly we are tired of compulsively seeking something that promises so much but delivers so little."[9] You're desperate to stop, and you may even have tried several times. But you keep coming back to porn. Or perhaps you have stopped the porn use, but the pull is still there. You haven't experienced wholeness.

Sheila received this email from a woman that shows what happens when we focus on quitting the porn rather than transforming our soul:

> When I got married I was so excited to explore sex with my husband . . . only to find that he wasn't. Fast-forward about a year and a half and a child later . . . he sits me down and tells me he has a problem with porn and has for a long time. Four years later and I'm still so hurt . . . I don't want to initiate because I hate what being rejected feels like. I just feel distraught. I love

him, but it's hard to trust him. I also asked him to tell me what it was that he was watching, and he refuses to tell me and told me that it's stupid that I even asked. I feel disregarded, lied to, left out, and manipulated. He's quit porn now, but I feel like he's just replaced it with video games, which is just as heartbreaking. It still puts me last.

Maybe this is your story. You've been using porn, and you got married thinking that your sex life could still be great—but it's not. How do you stop that snowball from rolling farther down the wrong side of the mountain? And how do you roll it back up so you can start again?

The answer won't be found in simply practicing better self-control. As Cusick says, "Following Jesus consists of so much more than trying harder and white-knuckling your way through it."[10] Jesus wants to lead us toward wholeness, not just sin avoidance.

The sin-avoidance model of quitting porn is the most commonly taught. You throw out the porn, you install filters on the computer, you find accountability partners to ask you the hard questions, and you share the passwords to your phone. Those preventative measures can be helpful, and when you're first quitting porn, filters can minimize the temptation, and sharing passwords can build trust with your wife. But these steps don't cure anything; they merely hit the reset button to allow you space to do the real work, preferably with a licensed counselor.

We need to go deeper and ask the hard questions. Why is porn alluring? Because it allows you to be with a fantasy of a woman without having to relate to an actual woman with needs of her own, who will want to see beyond your facade. It allows you a dopamine rush that feels like intimacy while allowing you to hold yourself back from your wife—and from God.

Healing comes when you stop hiding. It comes when you take your woundedness and your shame, the parts of you that you manage to push down with the porn use, and allow God, and even your wife, to see them.

That's why Cusick calls for accessibility rather than accountability. Accountability involves someone grilling you, making sure you're falling in line. Accessibility gives someone else access to your heart. You open up. You become vulnerable. You find out what's behind the curtain, and you share it with others. When you are truly seen, then the God who binds up your wounds can start to heal.

> Healing comes when you stop hiding.

Cusick went through many stages of recovery from sex addiction himself before becoming a counselor, and with each stage, more and more layers were torn back until he was able to be vulnerable and confront his wounds. A victim of child sexual abuse, he had layered years of porn use, combined with using prostitutes, to hide from his fear of being truly known. As he confronted his wounds, his PTSD from child abuse returned. He found that the only safe place when the flashbacks started was his walk-in closet, where he would curl up in a ball and wait for them to pass.

After one particular episode, he was listening for his heart rate and breathing to slow when the doorbell rang.[11] He heard the voice of his friend Eric, a twenty-year veteran of the police force. Then he heard something else that petrified him: he heard God telling him to invite Eric into the closet with him because God wanted to show love to Michael through Eric.

"But I'm almost naked," Michael told God. "There's snot running down my face, and I can't stop crying." But he felt God insisting.

Michael said,

> When [my wife] opened the door, I knew that my greatest desire—to be loved and accepted for who I really was—was deeper and truer

than my fear of being rejected. So I said to my wife, "Honey, please get Eric. I want him to see me." . . . As Eric slowly knelt down and rested his hand on me to comfort me, I had never felt so vulnerable, exposed, and naked. . . . In that moment I knew I had nothing to hide, nothing to prove. . . . The voice of Love began countering my lifelong voices of shame.[12]

Real healing from addiction isn't about trying harder and having more self-control. It's far riskier than that. It's peeling back the layers of protection you've built up over your life that have protected you and others from seeing the truth about you.

But God isn't afraid of the truth. He already knows it. And he loves you regardless, without limit. When you allow yourself to be truly seen by him, you will finally be able to start your journey toward wholeness. We pray you will seek out and find a licensed counselor trained in addiction recovery to help you on that journey. And we pray you will find your way to intimacy with your wife, perhaps for the first time.

STEPS TO REBUILD IN A RELATIONSHIP MARRED BY PORN

- Apologize and take responsibility for how you have hurt your wife, without being defensive.
- Earnestly and consistently seek the help you need around both aspects of recovery—accountability and accessibility.
- Restore emotional connection.
- Respect that your wife needs time to heal. Give her permission to set the pace for recovery.
- When and if you are both ready to reconnect physically, start with nonsexual touch.
- When you are ready to reconnect sexually, focus on the relational aspects of sexual intimacy. Say "I love you." Use her name. Maintain eye contact.

- Kiss deeply while you're making love to reinforce intimacy.
- If you feel images returning to your mind and you lose focus on your wife, stop what you're doing until you re-establish connection with her. Return to kissing, nonsexual touch, telling her you love her, massage—do whatever it takes to always make sex a personal and mutual experience.

CHAPTER 15

Beyond Bouncing Your Eyes

For decades, radio personality Paul Harvey ended his show with the iconic words, "And now you know the rest of the story." He would introduce a tale that initially sounded rather run-of-the-mill, but then he'd fill listeners in on fascinating background that changed everything. A young druggist tries to make a headache cure from a syrupy mixture and tells people to mix it with water. One day carbonated water is added by mistake—and Coca-Cola is born!

Well, here's a story you may have grown up with: Lust is every man's battle, and you have to honor your wife by not checking out other women, no matter how much you want to. You have to stop noticing all the boobs and butts that go by, even though you're hardwired to do so. And because you're male, this will always be a battle for you. Women can make that battle easier by not showing so much skin and by dressing modestly so they don't cause you to stumble. But above all, be vigilant. Be pure in your mind.

A lot of guys internalized that message and honorably try to live a lust-free life. And many, many guys are stressed about it. In our survey of three thousand men, 75.5 percent of guys report that lust is something they struggle with on a daily basis.

But now we'd like to tell you the rest of the story.

Let's go through a day in the life of one of those 75.5 percent of men who say they struggle with lust daily. In our survey, we asked about certain scenarios and how the men would deal with them. What would you expect to happen when a man who struggles with lust has a conversation with an attractive woman? Does he stress about it, worrying he will lust after her or feel awkward in her presence? Only 18.9 percent do.

What if he is out for breakfast with a buddy and a good-looking waitress with a low-cut top serves them? Would he stare at her? Of the men surveyed, 12.7 percent said they would. Would he try to capture her form so he can think about her later? Only 0.5 percent of men would. The vast majority (86.8 percent) go on with their eggs and bacon.

What if he pulls into a parking space at the grocery store and in front of him a young mom leans into a minivan to put her toddler in a car seat, with her backside on full display. Would he fixate on her rear? Only 3.8 percent of men would.[1] Fantasize about her? Another 0.9 percent of men would. The other 95.3 percent? They'd head into the store and work through their grocery list.

And finally, what if he's at church and an attractive fourteen-year-old walks in wearing a revealing outfit. Would this cause him to lust? Of the men we surveyed, 1.8 percent would feel an overwhelming temptation to lust, but the vast majority would simply notice her and then go on with their worship.

What is going on? We performed a survey of over three thousand men where three quarters told us they struggle with lust on a daily basis, but when scenarios were suggested where they might lust—in a social setting, in a restaurant, on errands, in church—very few report that they would! In fact, 70.3 percent of the men who say they struggle with lust report they would not actually lust in any of our scenarios. Could it be that the rest of them stated they had a problem with lust because they actually have a problem with porn? That certainly accounts for some of the discrepancy.

But even so, 55.8% of men who say they struggle with lust do not report lusting when given the chance and do not report having a problem with porn.

Now, it's not quite as simple as that (Paul Harvey's stories were never quite straightforward either). We found that 41.8 percent of men do report that they're tempted to lust on a daily basis by memories or porn or other women they've seen in the past. But only around 40 percent. Not 80 percent. Not 90 percent. Certainly not *every man*. But even more, is having unbidden thoughts that you don't entertain even a sin? Just because a memory of porn comes into your mind does not mean you've lusted.[2]

It looks like we feel an awful lot of stress about something that isn't as widespread a problem as we have been told. So where's the disconnect? We think it's mostly a definitional one.

What Does It Mean to Lust?

If you notice that a woman is beautiful, is that a sin? Have you already lusted after her in your heart?

If you read many bestselling Christian marriage books, you might say yes. If you notice a woman, then you will be tempted to undress her. You need to resist that temptation! So you need to avoid seeing her body. You need to "bounce your eyes," as *Every Man's Battle* tells you.[3] What if lust doesn't work that way? What if that's "criminalizing," for lack of a better term, *life*? And what if that approach misses an even bigger sin?

Noticing that a woman is beautiful does not mean you are automatically lusting and therefore sinning. Jesus said, "You have heard that it was said, 'You shall not commit adultery.' But I tell you that everyone who looks at a woman lustfully has already committed adultery with her in his heart" (Matthew 5:27–28).

Notice a few things about this passage. It does not say that everyone who *sees* a woman has committed adultery. It says that a man who *looks lustfully* at a woman has committed adultery with her. Seeing is not a problem. Seeing is inevitable. Looking, however, is done deliberately. But looking, in and of itself, is also not sinful. The problem comes when looking—the action—is paired with a certain mindset—with lust. Deliberate action plus a deliberate mindset.

Seeing is not the issue. Looking is not even the issue!

The issue is looking with the purpose of obtaining sexual gratification (even if it's just mentally).

Sexual attraction is a hardwired state of being over which you have no control. Sexual attraction falls under the *seeing* side of the equation. A person can find another individual attractive and not let that have any bearing on their thought life, their fantasy life, the condition of their marriage—anything! Finding someone attractive does not mean you are mentally cheating on your spouse. Noticing someone beautiful walking by does not mean you are lusting.

Think about how we handle anger. If someone says something insulting about someone you care about, you will naturally feel angry. That feeling in itself is not good or bad; what is important is how you deal with it. Do you give in to your base urges, or do you do the right thing? In the same way, noticing that a woman is beautiful or has an attractive figure is instinctual. It is not good or evil; it's just biological. It happens in a part of our brains we don't control. But once our conscious brain registers and starts to weigh in on the situation, we can handle ourselves in many different ways. That's where morality comes in.

Attraction is simply factual: *She has nice curves.* When you're in the factual realm, you haven't crossed any line. But once you move from factual to fantasy—*I wonder . . . Maybe I'll . . . What if . . .*—then you have crossed that line.

If you feel a bit of exhilaration because a woman's beauty surprises you, but then you go on with your day without it affecting you, that is not lust, even if you found her alluring. If you can look at that waitress and notice that she has a nice chest but then go back to your conversation with your buddy as you slather more jam on your toast, you haven't lusted.

Sheila was recording a podcast recently with a young host who said, "I was once walking on the beach with my brother, talking, when a really beautiful woman jogged by. We both were startled and turned to look, and said, 'Wow, she's gorgeous,' and then continued our conversation right where we left off and didn't think about her again. She was just really beautiful and we noticed, but that's all it was." Exactly.

When Sheila recently explained this concept on her podcast, one man wrote in, saying,

> It's very liberating to realize that noticing a woman is not lusting. It feels like a huge weight lifted off of me. I've been deeply frustrated over the years because it seemed near impossible not to lust. I've even thought that if I could give up my sexuality entirely just to be free of the guilt of lust, I would probably do that. I say that as a man who has a very good and mutual sex life with my wife. Realizing what lust actually is (and isn't) has helped me realize that living life with a pure heart is actually POSSIBLE, and not a cruel command from God. Thank you!

We've had so many signs on the top of that mountain pointing us in the wrong direction, teaching us to be hypervigilant, and it's led to shame and guilt. It's time to ignore those signs and turn in the right direction instead. Let's look at how to do that by reframing the problem.

What's the Root Problem with Lust?

Part of what we get wrong in our discussion of lust is that we frame lust as an assault on men's purity instead of an assault on women's personhood. Understanding how much lust hurts women can make fighting against it easier. Lust is a sin because it diminishes and degrades women, treating them as objects for a man's pleasure rather than people Christ died for. Whether it is lingering over her for your own pleasure or actively fantasizing, when you lust, you use her for your gratification rather than treating her as one who bears the image of God. Unfortunately, the church's traditional model of lust treats it as inevitable, as if lust is one step in the levels of attraction, like this:

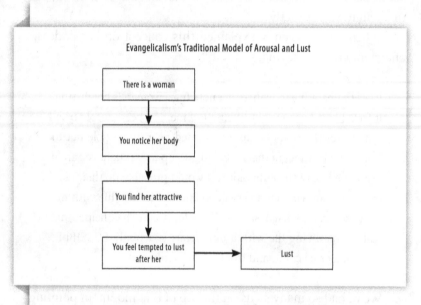

Lust is portrayed as a moving sidewalk—once you're on it, you can't get off. Once you notice that she has breasts, you're going to be attracted to her, which will make you tempted to lust, which will result in lust. So you have to nip it in the bud. You can't even notice her! That's stressful, because—no surprise—women are everywhere.

What we're suggesting is that the model of lust looks more like this:

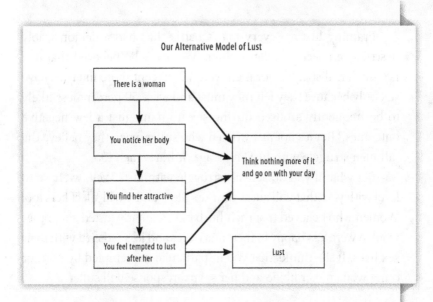

Our Alternative Model of Lust

There is a woman → You notice her body → You find her attractive → You feel tempted to lust after her

Think nothing more of it and go on with your day

Lust

We Need to Stop Framing Lust as Every Man's Battle

What would happen if we began to see lust more like the second picture rather than the first one? We'd find freedom, and we'd avoid the destructive consequences of the "all men struggle with lust" message.

How does a husband believing that lust is "every man's battle" affect a couple's marital and sexual satisfaction? (What percent more or less likely are they to experience the following?)

I have never had a porn problem	-74.7%
I am satisfied with my wife's level of enthusiasm in bed	-66.8%
My wife is satisfied with how frequently she orgasms during sex	-45.8%
I am satisfied with my wife's level of adventure in bed	-42.9%
My wife can communicate her sexual desires and preferences with me	-40.9%
I am satisfied with how frequently my wife orgasms during sex	-37.1%
My wife makes my sexual pleasure a priority during sex	-36.1%
I can communicate my sexual desires and preferences with my wife	-28.7%

Framing lust as "every man's battle" has had a demonstrably destructive effect on relationships. Women who believed that lust is a universal struggle for men were 79 percent more likely to have sex only because they felt they must and were 59 percent less likely to be frequently aroused during sex, to name just a few negative outcomes.[4] But it's not just women who suffer when they believe the "all men struggle with lust" message. It hurts men too.

But what if you do actively struggle with lust? Well, we have to level with you: that will affect your sex life—and it will affect hers too. Women who believed that their husbands regularly lusted after other women were less happy in their marriages and less satisfied with their sex lives. If she thinks that you in particular are tempted by porn or other women, her libido and her sexual response will suffer.

How does a wife believing that her husband is often tempted by porn or other women affect a couple's marital and sexual satisfaction? (How many times more or less likely are they to experience the following?)	
I am often afraid my husband will look at porn or other women	12.9
I engage in sex with my husband only because I feel I must	2.4
When it comes to sex, I could take it or leave it	1.4
I reliably orgasm during sex	-1.7
I am frequently aroused during sex	-2.1
My husband makes my sexual pleasure a priority	-3.5

If Every Man Lusts, Then Women's Bodies Are Dangerous

Also, by teaching that the struggle with lust is universal and is primarily a problem of men's eyes coming in contact with women's anatomy, at some level we teach girls that their female body is a source of evil.

For a woman to embrace her sexuality, she has to accept her body, which is a huge problem for many women who have been told since they were girls that their bodies are sources of shame and sin. Our own daughter was taken aside by a female youth leader when she started to develop. She gave her tips on how to dress in a way to avoid men lusting after her. That is unacceptable. Not only had she never dressed in any way that could be considered inappropriate, but also *she was eleven years old!* How did it ever become normal in the church to teach little girls that they are responsible to keep grown men from lusting after them?

Incidentally, men who believe the universal lust message are 2.5 times more likely to report being tempted to lust after the fourteen-year-old in our vignette than men who don't—which brings us to probably the most disturbing legacy of the lust message.

If Every Man Lusts, We Have Normalized Lewd Behavior

A few years ago, I (Keith) was shocked to see a video of Paige Patterson, then president of Southwestern Baptist Theological Seminary, telling a story during a sermon about a mother chastising her son and his friend for gawking at a sixteen-year-old girl.[5] The punch line comes when Patterson rebukes the mother because the boys were "being biblical." God made women beautiful, so men will naturally gawk.

Noticing may not be lusting, but choosing to gawk is certainly problematic. A gentle reminder that they were not being respectful toward this girl and an encouragement to a higher level of behavior would seem to be the appropriate response. Not only did Patterson *not* do this—even worse, he himself stated with rather disturbing relish that "she was (ahem) . . . *nice.*"

Clearly in this encounter, his own conscious mind was quite engaged as well. It was certainly engaged long enough that he imprinted a clear memory of the scene, yet at no point did he register that he was a sixty-year-old man and she was a sixteen-year-old girl. Public outcry made him eventually deliver an apology, but the fact that he could feel comfortable using this illustration in the first place shows how accustomed we in the church have become to the objectification of women.

By teaching that lust is a natural and inevitable response to seeing a woman, we equate male sexual desire with the objectification of women. Not only does that needlessly shame men for having a normal sexual drive when they have done nothing wrong; it also gives men a free pass when they are being creepy and inappropriate. "Oh well," we excuse them. "Boys will be boys." But not all men are like that. *And the ones that are don't have to be.* Men don't have only two choices: objectify her or don't even look at her. There is a third option.

> Men don't have only two choices: objectify her or don't even look at her. There is a third option.

A Healthier View of Male Sexuality

Jesus did not see women as objects but as people. He sat down and had conversations with them, even though that was taboo at the time. He talked with the Samaritan woman by a well when it was just the two of them, even though his disciples were aghast. But he valued her and had something he wanted to say to her. It was to that woman that he first revealed explicitly that he was the Messiah (John 4:26). And what about the apostle Paul? Paul called women his fellow coworkers and colaborers in the gospel. If Paul could work with women when it was taboo and Jesus could speak with women alone without lusting, then it should be expected that a man can interact with a woman and not lust.

You can choose to see women as whole people, created in the image of God and for whom Christ died. You can take every thought captive (2 Corinthians 10:5) and choose to see women in a way that respects their God-given dignity. You can go through life without lusting.

One man summarized it best like this:

> This message frees us from such a low childlike standard that has been taught often by the church. I literally thought for the first five years of my marriage that I had this incredibly impossible lust desire that I couldn't manage and expected my wife to give me sex and avoided women or scenarios that would tempt me. But now I feel more like an actual adult and can manage my emotions when I don't have my desires met instantly and have no problem dropping off a female coworker from work when she has car trouble without it being all weird for me.

Men, we are capable of treating women with dignity. And when we do that, women will feel safer. Women will feel valued. And our marriages will fare better than if we portray lust as a never-ending battle that we will always be fighting—and losing.

We've looked at everything that can steal intimacy from your sex life by distorting how you see sex and your sex drive. Now let's return to the bedroom and look at how to experience real passion!

CHAPTER 16

Adding Some Spice

A friend of ours likes to say that sex is a lot like pizza. When it's good, it's really, really good, but even when it's so-so, it's still pretty good.

Most of us guys enjoy sex, even if it's not particularly exciting that night. But just because we enjoy greasy all-cheese pizza doesn't mean we can't prefer a thick-crust meat lovers with jalapenos. Spicing things up can be fun!

But what happens when your idea of spicy and her idea of spicy collide? What if she prefers Hawaiian—the exact opposite of spicy, and kind of, well, fruity? That's what about half of you are experiencing, since in our surveys 49.1 percent of men reported being dissatisfied with their wife's sexual adventurousness. How do you turn up the spice in a way that honors her and creates passion?

It's Natural for Women to Be More Hesitant in the Bedroom

First, let's acknowledge that spiciness tends to be easier for men. Women need to concentrate more to feel pleasure during sex than men do, and they often find one position that works and want to stick with that. It's also women who, when more adventurous things are attempted, may be put in a literally uncomfortable position. "Will this hurt?" is a legitimate concern that guys don't share in the same way.

Plus, many of the more adventurous things we do in the bedroom have degrading associations for some women. Oral sex, for instance, is one of the most commonly used acts to sexually assault women, as well as one of the most commonly requested acts from prostitutes or depicted in pornography. Even though oral sex can be a healthy part of a married sex life (as we'll talk about in a minute), for many women, maneuvers like this have problematic associations. And if porn use or affairs have been a part of your history, then she may be even more hesitant to try anything out of the ordinary. How does she know you didn't get the idea from pornography?

Figure Out Why You Want More Adventure

When spicing things up, we have to go back to square one. What is the real reason you want more adventure? Is it so that you can increase the fun quotient in your marriage? Is it because you want to see if you can give her amazing orgasms? Or is it because there's a particular act you can't stop thinking about, and you feel you deserve it?

Great sex is always about experiencing something together and giving to one another; it is never about one person selfishly using another. Spicing things up has to be done not because you're dissatisfied with her but because you want to experience more of her.

> Spicing things up has to be done not because you're dissatisfied with her but because you want to experience more of her.

That's why even though putting the "spicy" chapter in the section on intimacy may seem weird, we decided to place it here because we want our guiding principle to be oneness and feeling close. Before you talk about spicing things up, ensure that you're honoring her with your motives. If you're battling porn right now, remember that she can't (and shouldn't) suddenly become a porn star to help you defeat that temptation. Rather, the more that she caters to those desires, the more she cements impersonal sex in your mind—and in hers.

The key to passion in the bedroom for her is *safety*—knowing that her comfort level matters to you, knowing that your relationship is safe and she doesn't have to perform to keep your interest, knowing that you love her and accept her as she is. When she has these reassurances, then passion can emerge. But if she senses that you will reject her in some way if she doesn't perform sexually the way you want, you will end up killing passion, not igniting it.

How Do You Decide What's Okay?

Let's turn to the parameters we've learned about sex to decide what activities are okay. God designed sex to re-create in a physical way the longing that we have to be joined to him. That longing is wrapped up in other issues: feeling loved and cherished, feeling intense pleasure, becoming supremely vulnerable. And in all that, there is no coercion. There is no fear.

Thus, for a sexual relationship to be able to express that spiritual connection, it can't be something that's scary or domineering, because God does not express his relationship to us that way. It's voluntary, but that doesn't mean it's tame! Let's look at some guidelines that logically follow:

1. You're married. You're allowed to do stuff! Freedom and liberty are themes of the Christian life (Galatians 5:1).

2. Sex should not be something that makes one person feel degraded or uncomfortable (Philippians 2:3–4).
3. If you or your wife don't want to do something, don't do it. Both parties must always be 100 percent willing, or you shouldn't do it (1 Corinthians 7:3–5).
4. Sex should always involve only the two of you. If you're fantasizing about someone else, or if she's fantasizing about someone else, it's wrong, even if you're physically acting it out with your spouse (see Matthew 5:28).

And finally, the one that sums up the whole thing:

5. Sex should be something that enhances intimacy, not detracts from it. What you do in the bedroom should make you feel closer, more known, more loved—not less known, less loved, or used.

How do we apply these guidelines to specific acts? Let's look at some of the most common questions.

What about Oral Sex?

We believe oral sex comes down to personal preference. Because sex is supposed to be something that connects you together, if anyone feels degraded or ashamed, it's not worth it. But if you want to incorporate it into your love life, we see no biblical injunctions against it. (Indeed, some make the case that Song of Songs 2:3, "his fruit is sweet to my taste," alludes to oral sex). And if she doesn't find the fruit "sweet to her taste"? Many women don't mind oral sex as foreplay but prefer not to have him climax in her mouth. Again, stick to her comfort level.

Remember that for most women, receiving oral sex is a more reliable route to orgasm than intercourse is. So oral sex isn't something you only *get*, it should also be something you *give*—if she wants it. If you're not comfortable with that? It's okay to say no, but then make sure you bring her to orgasm in other ways. And don't expect to receive something that you're not also willing to give.

What about Anal Sex?

While oral sex is more mainstream, anal sex is not, though its popularity is growing. We don't think the Bible speaks directly to the issue within marriage. Nevertheless, biblical injunction or not, we see anal sex in a very different category than oral sex.

Anal sex, after all, can cause injury. It comes with a higher risk of tearing and spreading disease. While the anus may be an opening in the body, the similarities with the vagina pretty much stop there. It's not like one's a front door and one's a back door; one may be a door, but the other is more like a sewage drain.

> Don't expect to receive something that you're not also willing to give.

And they're anatomically distinct. The vagina has many nerve endings; the rectum has few. The rectum is part of the digestive system and was designed to absorb material, which is why spreading disease is easier. The vagina has a low pH to kill germs; the rectum has a neutral to high pH. The vagina's epithelium is relatively thick and is highly elastic, whereas the rectum's is quite thin and less elastic. If you're going to engage in any kind of anal play, you have to be much more careful with cleanliness, and never switch from anal to vaginal sex without washing well or switching condoms, since spreading bacteria from the anus to the vagina can cause infections.

Ultimately you as a couple need to decide what is right for you, but you should clarify why it's appealing. Is it because you want to feel closer together, or is it because you've bought into what the pornographic culture says is sexy? If it's the latter, be careful you aren't feeding into a view of sex that's a hindrance to intimacy rather than a help.

Can We Use Sex Toys?

Again, we don't think there are specific biblical injunctions against sex toys like vibrators or rings or toys; freedom is part of a grace-filled marriage. But we must take this in the spirit of "Everything is permissible; not everything is beneficial" (1 Corinthians 6:12 BSB). Something may not be forbidden, but think and pray about it before you add to your marriage something that could drive you into an unhealthy emphasis on physical pleasure for its own sake rather than for the relationship's sake.

Also, many women lament that they can orgasm with a vibrator but not with their husband. Vibrators provide such intense, direct stimulation that no guy can compete with. And sometimes, when reaching orgasm is more difficult, the couple relies on a vibrator because it gets her there faster, rather than working at how to unlock her sexual responsiveness in other ways.

When sex toys provide a shortcut, they may inhibit intimacy because what most women want is to be able to orgasm from their husband's stimulation. If you struggle with getting her to orgasm, go back and read the "Physical Pleasure" section of this book again, doing the exercises to learn how to work through the sexual response cycle to get to arousal and orgasm.

Is It Okay to Masturbate?

First, let's define what we mean by masturbate. Touching your genitals is not necessarily masturbation. If you're touching yourselves during foreplay, if you're showing each other what feels good, if she puts her finger on her clitoris during intercourse to enhance stimulation—those are not masturbation. There is nothing magically forbidden about one's hands coming into contact with one's genitals.

And if you're debating masturbating because you're simply away from each other, maybe let each other in on it! That's a lot more fun (as long as she's comfortable too). Chances are you each have phones and can talk to one another. (Please beware of Skype or FaceTime on public Wi-Fi from hotels! Be smart. It's easy to hack those signals.)

Masturbation, as commonly understood, though, is bringing yourself to orgasm by yourself, without your spouse. This can cause problems when it is used as a shortcut to avoid doing something that could build intimacy. If you're turning to masturbation because it's easier to masturbate than to have sex with your wife, then you're stealing sexual energy from her because you'd rather not be bothered doing the work of making her feel good in bed. If your wife doesn't want sex often and you're turning to masturbation instead of figuring out why she doesn't want sex—and healing that rift—then you're using a shortcut.

Masturbation is easier than sex. When you masturbate, it feels more intense immediately, and you can bring yourself to orgasm without all that hassle of worrying about someone else's pleasure. But that changes the dynamic of sex. Sex was meant to be mutual. If sex is only self-serving, then it isn't about a knowing of another but instead about a selfish entitlement to release.

Sometimes it can feel like masturbation is a gift: she doesn't have much of a sex drive, and you do it so you don't bug her. But consider whether by masturbating you are allowing a bad situation to continue. Your wife likely doesn't want sex *for a reason*. Figuring out that reason and dealing with it should be the goal. God gave you your sex drives so that you would be drawn to each other. The uncomfortable feeling of sexual frustration can motivate you to work on your issues and to improve the relationship.

Now, sometimes masturbation *can* be selfless. Fertility tests in medical labs require masturbation, after all. But sometimes even within your relationship, masturbation can be a giving thing to do.

At a marriage conference, a woman approached Sheila to talk about how to navigate their sexual relationship when she was battling tremendous pain during sex (vaginismus), for which she was getting treatment. She was discouraged, depressed, and felt like a failure. The husband felt a buildup of sexual frustration, but the last thing he wanted was to burden his wife. He wanted to love her and let her feel unconditionally cared for as she pursued treatment. Is masturbation (to thoughts about his wife) in this case wrong?

He wanted to do it not to steal the sexual side of their relationship, but rather to protect her and help her feel loved and accepted while she was going through a time when she couldn't have sex. The couple was connecting in other ways sexually, but this too was sometimes difficult for her because she still felt like a failure. So she was orgasming at times but found the pressure to perform sexually to be daunting. If masturbation is something that allows you to be more giving in the relationship, that's one thing. But if masturbation is used simply to relieve sexual frustration while not initiating any intimacy with her, or as a way of avoiding dealing with issues in the relationship, then it's a problem.

Please don't take what we're saying to mean, "If I'm sexually frustrated, it's a gift to my wife for me to masturbate." What we're saying is more nuanced. We don't mean some Tuesday where she turns you down. We're talking about an extended period of time. If your wife is consistently rejecting sex and has a very low libido, the answer is working on the relationship, figuring out why she says no to sex, trying to rebuild your friendship, or even going for counseling. Don't use masturbation as a shortcut to avoid doing real work in the relationship.

What about Bondage and S&M?

There's a huge difference between tying someone up and teasing them so that sensation is heightened and tying them up and degrading them. If you have to emotionally distance yourself from your spouse to get turned on, or if degrading or humiliating someone else turns you on, that is a problem. That isn't real passion; that's counterfeit, and it's cruel, objectifying, and wrong. Playing and teasing are great! Humiliating is not. Communicate openly so that you each understand when that line is crossed for either of you.

What about Taking Sexy Photos or Videos of Each Other?

First, be careful if there are sex addictions in the past because taking photos and videos could easily cement such an addiction. If you require an image to get turned on, then you haven't defeated porn. That being said, many couples find this idea exciting and fun.

Our biggest concern here is the practical. What if tomorrow you were to die in an accident and your kids found these images? Or your best friend? Or your mom? What if the kids have the password for your phone and browse your photos? There are some pretty obvious privacy issues you need to be aware of and to consider carefully. Even outside the "is this permissible" issue, there's also a wisdom issue and a safety issue for your children (who don't ever, ever want to see that!).

Other Fun Ways to Spice Things Up!

In *31 Days to Great Sex*, Sheila's book for couples to spice up their sex life, she explains how the dice game works.

Get two dice of different colors, and write on a sheet of paper what each die means.

First Die—Actions

Choose six actions, like kiss, stroke, lick, rub, flick, suck, and assign them to the six sides of the die.

Second Die—Parts of the Body

Assign the six sides of the second die to six body parts, like mouth, fingers, ears, toes, genitals, breasts.

Take turns throwing the dice, and do whatever combination comes up! You can make the game as adventurous or as tame as you want by varying the actions or body parts. Make sure you give enough time—let's say at least a minute—to each task.[1]

Want to go even further with the dice game?

Instead of matching an action with a body part, assign a specific activity to each number on the die (you could do six or twelve or somewhere in between, depending on how many activities you want to use). Each of you assign activities to three numbers on the die—things that drive you wild (or if you want to use an eight-sided or twelve-sided die, then you each get more options!). These can be mild, like deep kissing or blowing and teasing and sucking his ear, or more adventurous, like watching her rub lotion on her breasts, performing oral sex, or using a specific sexual position. Then use a timer app on your phone, roll the die, and take turns doing each activity for two minutes. This constant starting and stopping delays orgasm for quite a while, so when it finally does happen, it's much more intense.[2]

Sheila has many more ideas in *31 Days to Great Sex*.

Fun Couples Keep Playing

Sheila and I have spent much of our time in our RV, traveling around North America, speaking, hiking, and bird-watching. One particular trip we were visiting a nature reserve in western Michigan, and as we stood up on a hill looking over a vast wetland, we saw two river otters making a ruckus. They would jump into the air, wrap themselves around each other, and slide down the hill into the water. Then they'd scurry up and do the whole thing again.

They were playing, as otters do.

Sex can be super serious. It says, "I love you." It's the quest for amazing orgasm. But it's also plain, well, *fun*. Just as pizza is good no matter what, so sex should remind us of its playful side. After all, sex is funny! Sometimes you squeak or make other noises when you don't mean to. But it's something special you share with only one other person. So don't stop playing and laughing. When you keep that attitude, spicing things up doesn't need to feel like some weird thing you do together that might verge on gross or frightening, but can simply be a continuation of the fun you have as a couple. And that's how it should be.

Part 3

PUTTING IT ALL TOGETHER

CHAPTER 17

When You Want More

For those of you who are too young to remember dial-up internet, here's how it worked. First you had to make sure none of your siblings or parents were on the phone line. Then you hit the button on your computer to connect and waited while it chimed and squealed for upward of a minute. Every time you went to a new page, you'd have time to go get a cup of coffee while it loaded.

And we found it amazing! We paid big bucks for it and considered it money well spent.

Fast-forward thirty years, and now when we use free Wi-Fi in Starbucks, if it takes longer than half a second for a page to load, we feel ripped off. What happened? How can we have more but feel less grateful? The answer: our expectations changed, as reflected in the saying, "A luxury, once enjoyed, becomes a necessity." Once we have something, we want it *all the time*.

In *The Good Girl's Guide to Great Sex*, Sheila included a "rah-rah" wrap-up chapter, encouraging women to prioritize sex in their marriage—because many husbands were frustrated with lack of frequency. In this chapter, we'd like to present the other side. Since frequency is the most common conflict in a couple's sex life, and since it's most often (though not always) because he wants sex more than she does, we need to talk about the husband's responsibility to create intimacy despite these libido differences. And that involves we men realigning our expectations with reality rather than with our emotions of the moment.

Here's what we want you to realize: *Treat a preference like it's a problem, and you'll end up with a problem.*

Let us explain. Our data shows that the more sex you have, the more satisfied you will be with the amount of sex you're having. Not exactly on par with the discovery of fire or the invention of the wheel, is it?

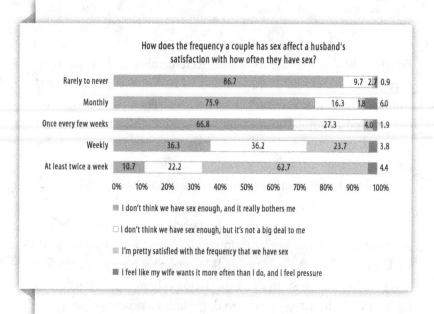

How does the frequency a couple has sex affect a husband's satisfaction with how often they have sex?

	I don't think we have sex enough, and it really bothers me	I don't think we have sex enough, but it's not a big deal to me	I'm pretty satisfied with the frequency that we have sex	I feel like my wife wants it more often than I do, and I feel pressure
Rarely to never	86.7	9.7	2.7	0.9
Monthly	75.9	16.3	1.8	6.0
Once every few weeks	66.8	27.3	4.0	1.9
Weekly	36.3	36.2	23.7	3.8
At least twice a week	10.7	22.2	62.7	4.4

- ▨ I don't think we have sex enough, and it really bothers me
- ☐ I don't think we have sex enough, but it's not a big deal to me
- ▨ I'm pretty satisfied with the frequency that we have sex
- ▇ I feel like my wife wants it more often than I do, and I feel pressure

What might be surprising, though, is that sexual frequency alone does not determine overall marital satisfaction. Sheila explained this in *The Great Sex Rescue*:

Research has found that frequency is not an accurate predictor [of marital satisfaction]—even for men.[1] Sexual satisfaction and interpersonal dynamics are far superior measures, as our survey also revealed. We found that how often a couple has sex is not directly related to their marital quality. However, women who are more sexually satisfied (who consistently orgasm and feel close during sex) reliably have better marriages. How happy your marriage is reflects the quality of your emotional and sexual relationship far more than it does the frequency of intercourse.[2]

Does that mean frequency doesn't matter at all? No, not exactly. It's just that the relationship isn't as straightforward as we may think. A study from York University in Toronto, led by psychology professor Amy Muise, found that more sex is better—to a certain extent. *Time* magazine reported her findings: "Muise and her study team found that couples who have a lot of sex tend to experience better wellbeing. 'Sex is associated with feeling more satisfied in a relationship,' Muise says. But beyond once a week, the wellbeing benefits of sex seem to level off. That's not to say that having sex a few times a week (or more) is a bad thing. It just doesn't seem to make couples any happier, she says."[3]

So frequent sex is good, but it's not *everything*.

And that caveat is key, because if we stress frequency at the expense of other indicators, we could end up creating a problem where there isn't one.

When Libido Differences Are Just Preference Differences

We wish we could put this in neon lights on that mountaintop: *lack of contentment with the frequency of sex, when sex is objectively relatively frequent, can create major problems in the long run.*

Let us tell you about a conversation Sheila had with Bob, who had been married for over forty years. He and his wife have sex once every six weeks, though Bob says it feels more like "duty sex," despite her consistent orgasm. Bob would love to bring her even more sexual pleasure and says he'd gladly sacrifice his pleasure for hers, but she's not interested. Sex is how he feels intimate, but she rejects it.

In the beginning of their marriage, she was "all over him," making love several times a week. She was also really orgasmic! But he could never understand why she didn't crave it more frequently. He'd announce, "We should do this more often!" or complain, "Why can't we do this all the time? It's so wonderful. Why don't you want it more?"

Another woman told a similar story:

I feel that I'm treading a fine line of our sex life being "satisfying enough" for my husband. He's the higher-drive spouse, and even though we have sex two to three times a week, he would prefer more. I do orgasm (through clitoral stimulation) almost every time. I think with the frequency, we rarely go long enough without sex for me to notice if I myself actually desire sex. . . . So it's hard to note my own natural libido or desire and stop sex from feeling like a duty.

Another woman said,

When we first got married, I did enjoy having sex, but it always felt like there were borderline complaints. He would tell me he wished the sex had been longer and he wished we would have it more often, and I felt like my comments were always opposite. I felt like it was plenty long (I don't have the time or energy for two or more hours of sex), and we were having sex at least every other day at first. With the complaints came a pressure that made me less interested.

Let's think about these three scenarios: In each case, the couples (at least initially) were having sex several times a week. In at least two of the three, the women were reaching orgasm. But in all three cases, the husbands were critical and expressed disappointment, even when sex was relatively frequent, telling their wives, "We don't do this often enough. Why don't you want it more often? This isn't enough."

In Bob's case, we see the result. The situation could have been different if Bob had expressed love, acceptance, and contentment rather than disappointment. Instead, because all he ever talked about was how sex could be more frequent, she felt inadequate. No matter what she did, she felt like it would never be enough. So she stopped trying to have sex frequently.

But What If Once a Week Honestly Doesn't Feel like Enough?

We'll address husbands who are in marriages where sex is even less frequent in a minute, but let's pause here for those of you who can relate to feeling frustrated with sex only a few times a week—or even once a week.

DO YOU SEXUALIZE EMOTIONAL NEEDS?

Sometimes men use sex to meet needs other than true intimacy. For instance, sex may help him:

- To feel more like a man
- To have a sense of control or to feel powerful
- To feel like he's important
- To bolster low self-esteem
- To reassure himself that he and his wife are "okay" as a couple
- To feel close without having to risk being vulnerable
- To deal with negative emotions such as stress, rejection, frustration, or anything that makes him feel inadequate

Many men are not trained in recognizing and handling emotional needs and instead sexualize them. This can result in a man feeling he has a high sex drive, when actually he is looking for sex to solve problems that it is not meant to solve. A healthy man learns to recognize and address his emotional needs outside the bedroom. When he does, often the desperately felt need for sex dissipates, replaced by a healthy drive for true intimacy with his wife.

Let's back up for a minute and ask a bigger question: Are we looking at sex from a consumer mindset rather than a relationship or intimacy mindset? Our consumer culture tells us we can't be happy unless we get everything we want and that to settle for less will lead to unhappiness later. If we combine that with a feeling of entitlement to sex, we create the perfect conditions for men to feel dissatisfied and for women who genuinely enjoy sex to want to run away from it. Andrew Bauman, a licensed therapist specializing in sex addictions and trauma, notes that the pornographic mindset impacts guys' dissatisfaction too:

> Pornography is always there, always ready and willing for me to orgasm—sex on-demand—so why should it be any different in marriage? When I have spent the entirety of my sexuality literally using women via screens whenever I want, these expectations are unconsciously transferred onto my real life relationships. Pornographic mindsets do not suddenly change after the wedding night. The expectations and demands are projected onto men's wives to compete with and fulfill the fantasies of the porn that they grew up indulging.[4]

This consumer mindset is incompatible with Christ-filled relationships. "The Son of Man did not come to be served, but to serve" (Matthew 20:28). Our lives should be about love, and love is not selfish; love is kind. Love requires contentment, which ultimately comes from our relationship with Christ: "I have learned to be content whatever the circumstances. I know what it is to be in need, and I know what it is to have plenty. I have learned the secret of being content in any and every situation, whether well fed or hungry, whether living in plenty or in want. I can do all this through him who gives me strength" (Philippians 4:11–13).

So let us ask this: Are you practicing contentment in your marriage?

What we have heard over and over again in our survey of twenty thousand women is that many, many women feel that no matter what they do, it is never enough. They start to think they can never satisfy their husbands' desires and soon wonder if there's even a point in trying. Sex, instead of being something she can joyously anticipate, becomes something where she's always seen as a disappointment.

Look, we understand many guys would prefer sex more often and can't figure out why their wives don't share their enthusiasm. But remember, if you're having sex twice a week or more, you're having sex more than the average couple. And if you're having sex once a week, you're only slightly below average. If your wife doesn't want sex every day or every other day, she is not rejecting you. It just means that there are other considerations as well, and part of loving your spouse is honoring what else is going on in her life.

> Many women feel that no matter what they do, it is never enough.

We're not saying you should aim for average. On the whole, we think that sex several times a week is healthier than sex once a week. But practicing contentment is also a discipline worth learning, both for your own well-being and for the long-term health of your sex life and your marriage as a whole. Expressing constant disappointment will only make the situation immeasurably worse in the long run.

When Libido Differences Are a Problem, Not Just a Preference

When your sex life isn't exactly as you would like it, focusing on contentment is the right course of action. But what if it's not that both of you want sex in healthy amounts, just to different degrees? What if frequency has dwindled to a few times a month or less and you're desperate to increase it?

Earlier we talked about the equation for libido:

$$\underset{\text{HEALTH}}{\text{EMOTIONAL}} + \underset{\text{HEALTH}}{\text{PHYSICAL}} + \underset{\text{SECURITY}}{\text{RELATIONAL}} + \underset{\text{CONNECTION}}{\text{EMOTIONAL}} + \underset{\text{SATISFYING SEX}}{\text{PHYSICALLY}} = \underset{\text{SEX}}{\text{WANTING}}$$

When one or more of those elements is missing, then libido will plummet. So now we need to ask some hard questions to see if something is affecting this equation. This may be a difficult exercise, but please pray and ask, "God, if any of these relate to me, please soften my heart so I can hear."

1. Have you been expressing frustration, anger, or criticism toward your wife?

If you were critical that your wife didn't enjoy sex or were frustrated that she couldn't orgasm or couldn't get aroused, it's likely that she now equates sex with something she's not good at. Or when she did have sex and enjoyed it, if you complained that you weren't doing it more, she may have internalized the message, "Nothing I do will ever be enough." If you focused on your own disappointment rather than helping her experience great sex, she likely picked up on it.

2. Did you take time to ensure that your wife felt pleasure?

When you were adjusting to intercourse, was her pleasure your focus? Did you slow down so that you could figure out what would arouse her, or did you assume that sex should feel as good for her as it does you, so it was her problem to solve? If you had sex for months—or years—without her experiencing pleasure or an orgasm, have you apologized? Maybe you wanted her to feel good, but she had too many hang-ups or wasn't comfortable with you trying to touch her. Even then, by going ahead when she wasn't enjoying herself, you may have solidified in her mind, "Sex is not for me."

3. Have you failed to honor her when she experienced physical issues that made sex uncomfortable?

Did your wife suffer from sexual pain, like vaginismus or postpartum pain, but you pressured her for intercourse anyway? Did you show her acceptance and love and reassurance, or did you talk about how disappointed you were to the point that she pushed herself to go through with sex because she felt so embarrassed and broken and guilty? If your wife experiences heavy cramping or heavy bleeding with her periods, have you expressed compassion for what she has to go through, or do you focus on your own sexual frustration?

4. Has sex been depersonalizing?

Many high-drive spouses say they feel most intimate with their spouse when they have sex, but then they have sex in a way does not build any intimacy for their spouse. Have you bought into a pornographic mindset (consciously or unconsciously), where sex is about using or "taking" someone, and not about "knowing" someone? Have you pressured your wife to do things she is not comfortable with and that don't feel intimate

> When women feel close to their husbands during sex, frequency increases.

for her or expressed disappointment that she won't try them? If you haven't been able to say "I love you" or say your wife's name during sex, but instead tend to use coarse language that your wife doesn't like, or even check out during intercourse so that it's obvious you're not thinking about her, then you may have turned sex into something ugly for her. Fifteen percent of women told our survey that one of their primary emotions after having sex is feeling used. If your wife feels this way, how likely is it that she will want sex? When women feel close to their husbands during sex, frequency increases.

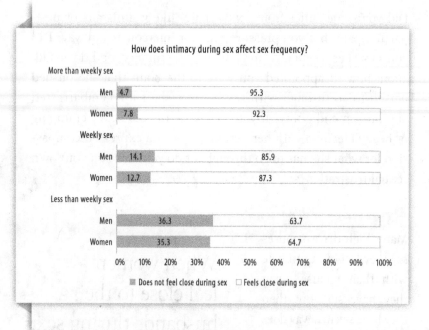

How does intimacy during sex affect sex frequency?

5. Have you broken trust with your wife?

If your wife has found you using pornography, or knows of a long-standing porn issue, then you have broken trust with her. If you have had an affair, either physical or emotional, and have not painstakingly rebuilt trust, then she may still be withdrawing. Repair the breach first before you worry about rebuilding sex.

6. Do you share the load with your wife?

If your wife is run off her feet caring for the family while you enjoy downtime, then she could simply be exhausted and feel taken for granted. If she carries most of the mental load for the family so that she has so many things running through her head that she can never "turn off," then maybe there's no room in her brain for sex. Some seasons in life are going to be busier and more difficult, like pregnancy or the postpartum phase or juggling exam season as a full-time student. Are you showing sensitivity during those times to care for your wife's needs?

7. Do you practice good hygiene?

The New Zealand comedy music group Flight of the Conchords has a hilarious song about married sex called "It's Business Time." In that song, they try to make normal tasks sound sexy, including brushing your teeth as a part of foreplay. But brushing your teeth *should* be foreplay! So should showering, if you have a job where you perspire a lot. And trimming a beard and fingernails makes oral or manual sex much more comfortable. Many women tell Sheila that their husbands' poor hygiene or lack of grooming is their biggest turn-off. This is such an easy one to fix, so rather than take offense, simply head to the bathroom.

8. Do you show your wife love outside the bedroom?

Does your wife feel loved, cherished, and valued outside the bedroom? Do you grope her or push yourself on her when she's doing the dishes, or do you show her affection in a way that honors her preferences? Are you kind and affectionate primarily when you want sex, and do you act disappointed and withhold affection if you don't receive it? Almost 18 percent of our respondents say their motivation for having sex is that their husbands are unpleasant to them if they don't. Over time, that has terrible effects on a woman.[5]

9. Are you emotionally vulnerable with your wife?

Many men who have a difficult time opening up emotionally prefer to have sex to connect. But sex is not a proper substitute for emotional vulnerability. Certainly this can be a "chicken and egg" thing—how can you open up to her when you feel sexually rejected by her? But to fix a problem, you can only change yourself and how you react; you can't change her. Practice sharing with her at the deeper levels of communication we talked about earlier in the book. We know that when both men and women feel close to each other, and feel as if they can communicate well, then they tend to want to have sex more often.

What If You See Yourself in Some of These Questions?

If you see yourself in some of these questions, take some time to pray through them, and ask God to show you how you have hurt your wife. You have not only pushed your wife away but also stolen the sex life that she was supposed to enjoy. Allow yourself to see the situation from her perspective and to feel the pain she has felt—even if she has caused you pain too.

Then tell her how you think this must have made her feel, even in a letter or email if that's easier than face-to-face. If you can remember specific times when you hurt her feelings, name those instances. Say, "I remember our anniversary two years ago when we were having sex, and I was using bad language. You asked me to stop and I didn't. Afterward I knew you were upset, but I didn't say anything. I think you probably went to sleep feeling used, and I'm sorry."

Ask her to forgive you, and commit to sincere and lasting change. Tell her that you know it may take her a while to trust you again, and that's okay. Prove you can be trusted by consistently treating her in a more Christlike way.

What If You Don't See Yourself in These Questions?

If you didn't see yourself in these questions, in some ways that's awesome. You haven't rolled that snowball in the wrong direction! But in other ways, this scenario poses its own challenges. If the problem isn't yours to begin with, then it's also not necessarily yours to fix.

Make sure that there aren't other issues that are launching that snowball down the wrong side of the mountain, such as your wife feeling stressed for other reasons: health issues, troubles with the kids, and so on. Do what you can to smooth out these issues. Then say to your wife, "I know we were meant for more. I want us to experience real passion and intimacy, but it feels like you continually push me away. That doesn't just make me sad, it also leaves me feeling rejected, lonely, and in despair. I don't want to live in a marriage like this, and I believe that we have to do something about it. We're missing out on so much. I know sex doesn't matter much to you, but I'd like to figure out how to show you what all the fuss is about. I am willing to do my part to make this the best experience it can be. Can we please try?"

And if that doesn't work, if it really is that she simply doesn't like sex and doesn't prioritize it, then talk to a licensed counselor. If she won't go, then go by yourself. A counselor can often help you see what's really going on and make a plan for how to address it.

■ ■ ■

When Geoff got married, he thought his problems would be over. Growing up with an alcoholic father, with no model of real intimacy, he thought that his loneliness and general sense of inadequacy would end once he had a woman beside him for life.

But instead it seemed like his problems intensified. He wanted her to help him feel like a man, but she looked for things from him that he had no idea how to give. Like many men before him, and many after him, he retreated into pornography. Intimacy seemed like a pipe dream.

They spent most of their married life fighting—fighting over money, fighting over the kids. Geoff felt like nothing he did was ever good enough. And the more he turned to porn, the louder her complaints got.

Finally, the downward spiral affected his work life, and he became serious about recovery, went to counseling, and joined a recovery group. He realized he had always thought his problem was sexual rejection. Instead, it was that he was running away from intimacy. He had been afraid to let his wife, Gail, truly see him. He wanted access to her body without giving her access to his heart. He was so full of shame that he thought that if she saw it, she'd retreat even more.

But as he learned to open up, it wasn't only his heart that was transformed. It was their marriage too. He found that for the first time in his life, he could pray with her. He wasn't always rushing to get to the next thing; he could sit quietly and enjoy a cup of coffee with his wife. And they started to enjoy an amazing sex life too! But sex was far less about a sexual hunger and more about a drive for connection. He started to feel whole.

Geoff's journey isn't finished. He knows he has much more to unpack. But he is passionate about calling guys to wholeness and to intimacy with their wives. Today he doesn't worry about his sense of inadequacy anymore. He's okay with Gail seeing the places where he doesn't always measure up—and seeing where he does! And together, they're finally experiencing real oneness.

Our hope is that as you deal with the underlying issues that drive you away from true intimacy with your wife, you'll rediscover libido together in a healthy way, as sex becomes a way to grow your life together, rather than just a need that has to be satisfied.

- Look for a licensed or registered therapist, psychologist, or social worker. Licensing means that they have been trained in evidence-based therapies, and they have ethical and professional guidelines they must adhere to, including protecting confidentiality.
- It's important for counselors to respect your religious views, but be careful not to assume that because someone calls themselves a "biblical" counselor that you will receive better therapy. Many biblical counselors are not trained in evidence-based therapies, and some are opposed to proven treatments (such as medication for depression) because they don't feel they are "biblical."
- Ensure that the counselor has specific training in areas that you need, such as trauma therapies if you're dealing with past abuse, addiction training if you're dealing with substance-use issues, or sexual addiction training if you're dealing with pornography use.
- Look for online reviews, and make sure to Google any counselor before you see them.
- Many counselors will offer a free phone twenty-minute consult so you can see if they're a good fit.
- If your local area has no counselors, many now offer counseling online.

Final Thoughts
The Truck Stop and the Five-Star Restaurant

Many summers ago, when our children were away at summer camp, we escaped for a week to the Couples Resort, a posh getaway near Algonquin Provincial Park in southeastern Ontario. Everything about that resort shouted "sex," from the logo of a couple intertwined to the huge king-size beds and Jacuzzis. We mentioned to a few friends in our hometown that we were headed there, and they all had the same somewhat puzzling reaction: "Oh, you're going to love the food!"

The first day we played a ton of tennis, took some kayaks out on the lake, and spent the afternoon doing other physical activities. By the time dinner rolled around, we were salivating, looking forward to this meal we had heard so much about.

To begin the evening, the waiter presented us with the tiniest little nibble to "whet your appetite." It was tasty, but it was only a single bite. When the menus arrived, with seven courses to choose from, Sheila found one of the options confusing. It said *scallop*, and we both wondered if the typesetter had forgotten the final s on the word. But she ordered it, and the tastiest scallop she could imagine arrived. But it was just *one*. The wild mushroom and beef consommé, the pâté and melon on greens—those were rather size-challenged too. Just enough was presented to seduce our taste buds.

While they were delectable, as the second and then third

courses arrived, I found myself feeling a bit desperate. Sure, the food was scrumptious, but each course was hardly enough to fill up a squirrel.

In my mind, I pictured the 10 Acre Truck Stop near our hometown, where we sometimes take my parents for lunch. You can order a cheeseburger platter that's enough to feed a small country, and if you gobble it down with a huge side Caesar salad, they basically have to roll you out afterward in a food coma. I thought, "I could really go for a cheeseburger platter right about now."

Yet by the end of the seventh course, we found ourselves deliciously full, even if it had taken longer than usual. It occurred to us that this five-star resort's goal was to make an *experience* out of eating. They weren't trying to fill us up; rather, they were maximizing enjoyment with each course while also whetting our appetites for what would come next. Because there was a lag between courses, by the time the next course came, we were ready for it and loved it!

As we end this book, we want to leave you with this picture of the dichotomy between the resort and the truck stop. Too often we see sex like a truck stop diner instead of like a gourmet resort: *I'm hungry. And that's a problem.* We try to see how much we can eat and how fast we can eat it so that we go as long as possible before we're hungry again. Sex becomes utilitarian.

If that's our attitude, though, then we're missing out on the beautiful experience sex was meant to be. Making love is not only about the response to physical urges, although it is about that. It's also the impetus to build deep, intimate connection in your relationship. It shouldn't be shoveled down; it ought to be savored.

We must abandon the truck stop mentality of sex in favor of the five-star restaurant mentality. Sex needs to be something that *awakens* hunger, not only something that satiates it. God created sex to be an integral part of our relationship, not only to satisfy a need but also to celebrate and reaffirm our union. When we eat simply so we aren't hungry anymore, the purpose is to make the hunger go

> ## Sex needs to be something that *awakens* hunger, not only something that satiates it.

away so we can get on with our "real" lives. But a sexual relationship that is a deeply intimate, emotionally close, and mutually satisfying "five-star" experience can be our real lives if we want it to be and we work to make it happen.

Let's not lose touch with reality, though. We're not arguing that every time we make love it has to be some mind-blowing experience where the earth moves. Life isn't like that. Each individual encounter may not be earth-shattering, but the sum total of the relationship should reflect that deep, intimate experience. And let us suggest that when we make love in the context of a Christian marriage, with God at the center, our relationship *should* reflect that. What makes it stupendous isn't only our feelings during each sexual episode but also the fact that we are joining more than just our physical bodies—we are joining our very selves. That joining is blessed and a blessing.

So sometimes you'll make love simply because you're anxious, on edge, or tired, and you need something to help you calm down. Sometimes you'll make love because you want to give her a gift even though you're pretty zonked yourself. Sometimes you'll have a quickie because the kids will be up in a minute and you're racing the clock. And sometimes you'll make love because you're incredibly aroused after thinking of something amazingly hot that you did together on vacation last year. It all merges into something that's personal, intimate, and so satisfying.

That's great sex. And you can give that to each other.

So what are you still doing here?

Appendix 1

Getting Ready for the Honeymoon

Let us tell you a tale of two honeymoons. One guy wrote,

> We had a special but low-key honeymoon. It wasn't long enough or where we really wanted to go—basically a long weekend in a small town about three hours away because I couldn't get vacation time—but the bonding was great! It took a while to figure things out, and we fumbled around a lot, but we tried all kinds of new things. Honestly, though? The best part was just not having to say goodbye at the end of the night. And realizing that this was only the beginning!

At marriage conferences, on Sheila's blog, and on social media, we've asked hundreds of couples over the years, "If you could do your honeymoon differently, what would you do?" The ones who said, "I liked our honeymoon!" tended to be like this first guy. They didn't go on a huge trip that left them exhausted. There weren't expectations for the trip of a lifetime or for gymnastic sex. They were simply happy to finally be able to be together and fumble through and have fun, even if it was a bit awkward.

But then there's the other, all-too-common story, as this woman expressed: "So we had sex because I thought we 'had to' or there'd be something wrong with us, even though we were exhausted and it was technically 1:00 a.m. the next day. Still enjoyable, but it would have been more enjoyable after some sleep!"

Many couples report putting pressure on themselves to "do the deed," and that tended to backfire—more so for some couples than others, as this woman explains: "[If I could do it over] I would speak up and say how tired and stressed out I was from the wedding day and would have slept and relaxed. I definitely would not have allowed myself to be subjected to three minutes of thrusting without arousal. It was bewildering and sad."

Bewildering and sad? Yikes! We don't want that for you. And the wonderful thing is that avoiding this scenario is not difficult. It all comes down to one big piece of advice: *don't put pressure on yourselves.* Relax. The couples who focus on relaxing tend to have honeymoons they remember with smiles on their faces.

Put pressure on yourselves to have an awesome honeymoon, or even awesome sex, and you might get the exact opposite. So throw out the word *should*—*we should have sex on our wedding night, she should reach orgasm right away, sex should feel great, we should have sex several times a day, this should be the most fantastic sex of our lives.* Get to know each other and have fun together, and let things unfold naturally. When Sheila and I got married, we thought that because we technically *could* have sex now, we had to achieve everything right away. And it backfired big-time.

In this section, we'd like to set up you guys who aren't married yet to have a great honeymoon. Let's start with some basic logistical info before we move on to sex.

Book a Checkup

Talk long beforehand about what form of contraception you will use—or if you will use any at all. And don't leave the decision or responsibility all to her. Shoulder the load with her.

If you've been sexually active before, arrange to get tested for sexually transmitted infections (STIs). Physicians are trained in providing treatment for and helping people deal with STIs and their effects. If you do have an STI with no curative treatment (for example, herpes), your physician can let you know about ways to decrease the chance of spreading it to your wife. If you pass something to her, it can impact her health, her fertility, and her comfort, so don't stick your head in the sand. Start your marriage with responsibility and honesty.

Think Exhaustion

What's the most important part of the honeymoon to you? Is it getting used to married sex? Or is it taking the most amazing, memorable trip ever? If it's the

> Exhaustion and amazing sex don't go together.

first, your honeymoon may not be the best time for a week-long hike in the Grand Canyon or a trip to Italy. It may be better to plan something low-key and closer to home, where you have time just to lounge around without being exhausted by travel and jet lag. You can always take a great trip on an upcoming anniversary.

If you plan on enjoying a relaxing and fun wedding night with your bride, then don't party until two o'clock in the morning at the reception. On the other hand, if you want to party late, go ahead! But change your expectations for what you'll do together when you get back to the bedroom, because exhaustion and amazing sex don't go together.

Don't make unrealistic plans that sound fun in theory but will actually be exhausting. One newlywed told us, "I wish we had stayed the night at a closer hotel instead of traveling the full eight hours straight from the wedding and arriving at our destination at six o'clock in the morning. I think a wedding night would have been even nicer than a wedding morning!"

One last bit of advice about the reception: lay off the alcohol. You will be at one of the biggest parties of your life, and if there's wine on the table or an open bar, you may be tempted to partake a lot. But a full 10 percent of the women we surveyed reported that they didn't have sex the first night because their husbands passed out from drinking too much. Definitely not a highlight for a wedding night.

Be Prepared for Her Period

It may be that your wedding date will be settled by circumstances outside your control—for example, when the venue is available. But if you do have some latitude and your fiancée's period is somewhat regular, you can pick a date to avoid it. Remember, though, there are no guarantees. If your fiancée's period arrives the night before the wedding, you might be disappointed, but trust us—she'll be more disappointed than you. She's the one who has to wear a white dress when she's worried about bleeding! Some women find their libidos are high during their periods, and they want to try sex anyway, while some find the cramping and the excess blood flow make anything sexy uncomfortable. Show compassion, and take things at her pace on the honeymoon.

Bring Lubricant

Sex is much easier for her, and much more comfortable for both of you, if she's well-lubricated. When women are aroused, their bodies naturally produce fluid that makes them "wet." But when they're nervous, lubrication can be more elusive. Two important fixes: first, spend a lot of time on foreplay, and don't rush intercourse. Second, buy some water-based lubricant and bring it with you.

Pack Pajamas—And Stuff to Do!

Pack pajamas. We'll let this honeymooner explain: "I didn't pack pajamas because I assumed we'd be sleeping naked or in sexy underwear, but the hotel room was freezing! It's my number-one advice to nearly-weds: bring pajamas, even if you don't think you'll need them!"

Yep. And we suggest that you fill up that suitcase with more than just lingerie and lube. If you're going somewhere for a week, you can't have sex constantly for seven days straight. Bring some books. Bring some board games. Bring hiking gear or skis or fishing poles. Create memories outside the bedroom too.

Now, let's turn to the sexy stuff—and the sexy expectations. We'll start with the most common question.

Do We Have to Wait Until the Wedding?

Does God require me to wait until I'm married to have sex? Is it a sin if we have sex first?

We believe that "Is it a sin?" is the wrong question. We think these are better questions: "How can I live out the kingdom of God with my fiancée and do what reflects Christ's ways? How can we do what is wise?" Often we frame sex before marriage as though God will love us if we wait and will be angry if we don't. But we believe that God's intention is that we reserve sex for marriage because he's a protective God who wants our best.

God made sex for multiple reasons: to have babies, to help us feel close to each other, and to feel great. All of these are better in marriage. Practically, marriage ensures that any children who come along are part of a lifelong relationship where they can be cared for. As well, when you commit to each other in marriage before having sex, the sexual relationship benefits from the foundation of an emotional and spiritual connection that is already there. Couples who have sex early in their relationship may *feel* strongly that they are connected because of those bonding hormones and having shared such an intimate experience. But one can mistake sexual intimacy for emotional intimacy and gloss over gaping holes in other areas of a relationship, failing to realize how shallow it is. In contrast, when you delay sex till after marriage, you naturally spend the lead-up time growing closer to each other emotionally and spiritually and building a strong friendship. Sex alone can't hold a marriage together. You will need that emotional and spiritual connection.

That's not to say waiting won't be difficult; it probably will be. And it *should* be. If you love her and feel close to her, you will naturally want to have sex with her. Take appropriate measures to make it easier rather than harder to resist those impulses. Try not to be alone together too late at night or hang out lying down on a bed. But remember that rules alone can't help you withstand temptation. This has to be a decision you make together with good reasons—so that you can grow other parts of your relationship before marriage, so that you can foster self-control, and so that you can be sure this is the right person for you.

On the other hand, if you don't feel at least some degree of sexual frustration while waiting, we have to ask some difficult questions: Are you sexually attracted to your fiancée? Do you have a sex drive at all? (Some people are asexual, meaning that they don't desire sex in any way.) Are you same-sex attracted instead? If you don't have any sexual feelings toward her, then that needs to be acknowledged before the wedding. Sex is only a part of marriage, but it is important. You may talk about this issue and decide to marry anyway, but it should be out in the open now. And we recommend you discuss this with a licensed counselor before marriage.

What If You're Already Having Sex?

When Natalie was dating her husband, she knew he'd had sex with other women before. She loved him and wanted to keep him and figured that he expected sex with her. So they became sexually active.

Maybe in your relationship you're already sexually active too. We'd like to give some serious advice here. Consider stopping until the wedding. You may figure, "What's the point? The horse has already left the barn! I'm not a virgin anymore." But virginity is not the point. Virginity is a state of being. God doesn't say, "Being of one state is a sin, but being of the other is not." God says, "I want you to act like this." It's not about whether you're a virgin; it's about what you choose to do today.

When you decide to stop having sex, you tell your fiancée, "I love you no matter what. I don't just love you for sex, I love you for you. I'm marrying you for you." That gives her more confidence in your commitment to her. And when you stop having sex, you also say, "I want to work on our intimacy and emotional connection, not just on sex. I want the foundation to be strong." And finally, you show her, "I am capable of waiting. I am capable of self-control." You're going to need that after you're married too! There will always be times when sex is off the table, like after childbirth or over work trips or during family crises or illnesses. Showing her with your actions that you can love her faithfully without sex, without turning to porn or other women, and without getting grumpy is an amazing gift.

What if she's the one who wants to keep having sex? She should still respect your boundaries. If she doesn't, that is a red flag that something is up, and you should speak to a licensed counselor together.

Disclose Your Sexual Past

Maybe you've had sex in the past, maybe she has, or perhaps both of you have. Please hear us on this: "having a past" does not necessarily mar your future. We know many guys who have married women with pasts (or vice versa), and it hasn't significantly impacted their marriage. We also know plenty of couples where one of them can't get over their spouse's past, and it continues to haunt them decades later. What puts some couples in the first category and some in the second?

Healthy couples deal with their baggage before marriage. They tell each other what they need to, but they reassure their beloved that it is in the past. How much do you reveal? A good rule of thumb is this: don't give enough detail that they could picture anything. Yes, it's important to know general numbers: Are we talking about one person? Five people? Dozens? It's important that they know the nature of the relationships: Were these long-term monogamous relationships? A series of hookups or one-night stands? And it's important to know the nature of the sexual encounters: Were they coerced? Was sexual assault involved? Or were they consensual?

If sexual assault or promiscuity was a part of your story or hers, seek out a licensed counselor and work through anything that needs to be dealt with. Often promiscuity is a trauma response and may signal that something else is going on that needs to be looked at. Full recovery doesn't always happen before marriage, especially when trauma is involved. But it's important to be on a good trajectory and to go into marriage with your eyes open—and with wise counsel.

Your fiancée also deserves to know if porn use is a part of your past—or your present. Porn habits can have a toxic impact on a couple's sex life, *and marriage will not cure a porn addiction*. But porn use doesn't necessarily doom your sex life; many guys use porn but put it behind them and recover. You should be free of porn for at least a few months before you walk down the aisle. Don't promise that you'll change *afterward*; rather, show your dedication *beforehand*.

Finally, don't marry someone if you can't accept their sexual past. None of us is perfect. When you say those vows, you promise to love each other completely, and that includes who they are despite—or even because of—their past. If you can't accept that, it

> Don't promise that you'll change *afterward*; rather, show your dedication *beforehand*.

is unfair to marry her and then hold it over her head as if she robbed you of something. Either marry her wholeheartedly, or leave her the freedom to marry someone else who can.

For Guys Who Haven't Had Sex with Their Fiancées

Will I Hurt Her If It's Her First Time?

Here's what women report:

"The first time doesn't hurt."

"It is sooo painful."

Guess that didn't clear the issue up much, did it? I suppose we should conclude that the correct answer is, "It depends."

Most women experience at least a slight sting when the hymen, the layer of skin that partially covers the opening of the vagina, breaks. If she's aroused, it's not that it doesn't hurt, but she often just won't care that much! Because she's the one who might feel discomfort, go at her pace. Typically, any pain felt is abrupt, and then it's over. Some women bleed a bit when the hymen breaks, and some don't. Make sure you have a towel nearby to protect the sheets. If she doesn't bleed, that doesn't mean you didn't do it right, and it certainly doesn't mean she wasn't a virgin. Believe your wife, not the bedsheets! Some women tear their hymens earlier in life without realizing it.

Even after the hymen is broken, women may take a while to feel comfortable in different positions. She may be able to have intercourse comfortably with you on top, but if you try something different, it may feel tighter, and she may need to get used to it.

If she experiences pain with penetration, then stop. Many women report some difficulty relaxing the first time, especially if they're scared it's going to hurt. If you can keep exploring and keep the situation "light," then that fear may subside. One woman, who suffers from a chronic pain condition and married in her thirties, told us,

> I was told premarriage by my doctor that sex would be extremely painful for the first few times (great, thanks!), but I'd say the worst I had was a little bit of soreness/stinging/burning—nothing bad enough to describe as "pain," never mind "extreme pain." And I reckon the reason why is because we did take it slowly and I was always aroused when we tried to do anything. I'm guessing he reckoned it would be extremely painful because he didn't think any couple would take things as slowly as we did! Just go really slow and steady!

That's great advice.

It's not uncommon for couples to take a week or more before penetration is comfortable. If it's difficult, don't keep trying repeatedly. Take a hiatus, have some fun in other ways, and circle back in a day or two. It's often easier to learn to bring each other to orgasm in other ways first, which also helps you become more familiar with each other's bodies. And most women who experience some pain at first do find that it resolves in a few days. So seriously—don't panic!

But if penetration continues to be painful, see a physician. She may have a thicker hymen that needs to be surgically removed (which is rare), or she may suffer from vaginismus.

Why Taking Things Slowly Is Important

Remember the book Sheila read before we were married that she ended up drowning? Well, before she drowned it, she read detailed, step-by-step instructions on what we were supposed to do on our honeymoon to bring her to orgasm the first time having intercourse. It made her a nervous wreck![1] It turned sex from something she had been looking forward to into a performance-based pass-or-fail test. Instead of sex being a journey of discovery we were going to take together, it became a formula that was being imposed on her.

So she froze. Sex was painful and difficult.

I wish before we had walked down the aisle, I had been told something like that could happen. Instead, it hit me out of the blue. How did the woman who seemed so attracted to me before we got married instantly turn into one who didn't want me at all? If I had known beforehand about vaginismus, then maybe I wouldn't have taken it as a rejection. I now realize that my feeling rejected had more to do with my own immaturity and selfishness, but it would have been so much easier to see that at the time if I hadn't received messages like, "If you wait till you are married, you will be rewarded; it will be amazing!" Those messages massively built up my expectations and turned sex into a personal reward for me, feeding my natural selfish tendencies. And my selfishness caused tremendous destruction in the first years of our marriage.

We want to stress that *most of you will not experience this*. Yes, our survey found that 22.6 percent of women suffer sexual pain not related to childbirth at some point, and around 7 percent of women experience it to the extent that penetration is difficult or impossible. But most do not. We tell our story, even though it's rather embarrassing and personal, because we know that primary sexual pain is more common among conservative religious couples, *and we think we know why.* And we think we have a suggestion to make it far less likely.

One of the findings from Sheila's survey is that women who were virgins on their wedding day are 25.1 percent more likely to experience vaginismus than women who had sex with their now-husbands before the wedding.[2] In talking with these women and in asking some follow-up survey questions, we found that one factor seems to be that they rush to intercourse because they feel like that's what they're supposed to do, skipping the natural sexual progression that gets them aroused. And when women have sex when they aren't aroused, it can be uncomfortable.

Having sex for the first time on the wedding night also adds another complication: you're having sex *because you're supposed to.* Even when a woman wants to have sex, doing so "on demand" because she's supposed to can feel like she doesn't have a choice. The feeling that this is something she *must* do, no matter what she feels like, is highly implicated in vaginismus.[3]

So give her back her choice. Let her know you're comfortable waiting until she feels aroused. Tell her before the wedding that there are no expectations—you have a lot of time to figure this out! Some couples will become aroused and excited on the first night, and others may take a few days or even weeks. But you'll end up in the same place. If we had waited the days or weeks until Sheila was truly ready and didn't feel pressure, rather than plowing ahead, we truly believe we would have saved ourselves years of heartache—and that's the story the numbers tell too. Explore each other's bodies. Discover how each other works. Try to bring her to orgasm in another way before you even attempt intercourse. That abides by the body's natural sexual progression, and it's more likely to work out well in the long run, while also honoring your wife's safety and comfort. Get comfortable together, work on arousal, and then you can turn to orgasm and intercourse!

One woman told us about how nervous and shy she felt on her wedding night: "I asked him to hold me instead of looking at me as my dress hit the floor. He did. And he still talks about that!" She felt cherished because he went at her pace, and they both enjoyed themselves.

Jenny also talked to Sheila about her wedding night. She and her husband, Jared, were scheduled to fly out early the next morning for their honeymoon. But they had also decided not to kiss until the wedding. Going from not kissing to having sex when you're exhausted and have to be up early the next morning? Leading up to the wedding, Jenny thought, "That's a lot for just one night!" But Jared told her, "I'm not a caged animal that's suddenly going to go wild when let free. Let's take our time and explore with no expectations." That's what they did, and the freedom to wait for sex until they got to their destination helped Jenny enjoy herself so much more.

What If It's Not Your First Time?

Most couples—even Christian ones—getting married today have had sex before marriage, either with each other or with someone else. Make your honeymoon special! Bring candles and massage oil. Draw out the experience, and feel what it's like to make love for the first time to the person you will spend the rest of your life with.

If you've had sex before but she hasn't, don't assume that you know what you're doing. She is her own person. Not every woman has the same likes. Let her body set your timetable, and make this

> If you've had sex before but she hasn't, don't assume that you know what you're doing. She is her own person.

into a journey of exploration where you discover not only how to have sex well but how to make love to your wife well.

Keep Sex in Perspective

Couples often have honeymoon fantasies about a magical night filled with gymnastic, passionate sex. But remember that the wedding *night* comes after the wedding *day*, which is the longest and—quite likely—one of the most stressful days of your life! And stress can seriously sabotage the sexual response cycle. Plus, the expectation that somehow on your wedding night you will arrive at "sexual nirvana" puts so much pressure on the two of you. We're not trying to dampen your enthusiasm about being with your wife. But we do urge you to see your wedding night and your honeymoon not as an arrival but as a departure, a beginning. You're about to *start* your journey, not finish it. And it is a journey that will get better and better as time passes.

> See your wedding night and your honeymoon not as an arrival but as a departure, a beginning.

Your honeymoon should be like Cape Hatteras. You're getting your feet wet, you're starting the journey, venturing out slowly—but there's so much more to explore. And you have a lifetime to do it.

Too many guys think of the honeymoon like a crack in the Hoover Dam. You've been holding back for so long, and now you don't have to hold back anymore! So it's going to be thunderous, awesome, and powerful. This mentality needlessly sets people up for disappointment if sex isn't perfect the first time.

Even worse, if the honeymoon is the pinnacle of sexual experience, then the only logical conclusion is . . . *it's all downhill from here.* Hopefully, the honeymoon will not be the pinnacle of your sex life. It may be amazing, and we hope it is, but either way, you have so much time to explore and enjoy afterward.

And that's the point: exploration, not destination. Instead of trying to "achieve" great sex, remember the real aim: to get to know your new wife in a whole new, very significant way and to allow her to see you in a whole new, very significant way. And we don't mean just seeing you naked. We mean seeing who you each really are.

That's what the guy in this story tried to do. His wife explains:

A week before the wedding, I was at the apartment, unpacking. He had just walked in the door when he caught me putting things away that I received at my "personal shower." I froze because we were in direct line of sight of each other, and I was holding a sheer nightie.

He put his work things down, stood in the doorway to the bedroom, and asked what it was. A little embarrassed, I told him it was my nightie for the honeymoon. He wasn't happy with my answer, and I couldn't figure out why. So I asked if he liked one of the others that weren't so sheer, and showed him. He then asked about the Tasmanian devil shirt that was once his and I claimed when we first started dating. He said, "I'd rather you packed that and left the rest."

I was so confused. On the way down to our destination, I asked him about it. He said, "Those things aren't you. They're not how I see you, and I know they make you uncomfortable."

She ended the story by saying, "I think I picked a good one."

Take your time on your honeymoon. No "shoulds." Just live in authenticity with each other, being the real you. For some that will mean sexy lingerie and rose petals and Jacuzzis. For some it will mean hunting cabins and bonfires and s'mores. It doesn't matter, as long as it's what you both want, where you both will feel relaxed, and where you'll be able to start the journey of your life together.

Then she'll know she picked a good one too.

Appendix
2

Discussion Questions

For Engaged Couples

This book comes with a companion book for your fiancée—*The Good Girl's Guide to Great Sex*! Ideally, have her read her book, and then, after you're both finished, set aside two or three blocks of time to discuss these questions together.

Preparing for Marriage

1. Does your partner know your sexual history? Take some time to share in general terms about how many partners you've had, whether those encounters have been in long- or short-term relationships, and whether they have been consensual or not. Allow your partner to ask any questions they have, but remember that you should not answer anything that might allow your partner to picture something explicitly. Talk about how you will put your sexual past (if any) behind you, and assure each other that the past is truly in the past.

2. Do you intend to use contraception? If so, each of you think of the method you are most drawn to, and then talk about this with each other. Do you have reservations about what your spouse wants to do? How will you decide what to do?

3. What do you want to do about sexual activity before the wedding? If you intend to wait for sex until you're married, make practical plans for how to make this easier. If you have been sexually active, does one or both of you want to stop? Are you honoring each other's boundaries?

4. Has porn or erotica been a part of your life? How much has this affected your view of sexuality? Is either a part of your life now? What are your plans to deal with this?

5. Have you experienced sexual abuse or other trauma in your past? Have you sought help and treatment for it? Your partner needs to be aware of any trauma you have suffered. If you have never disclosed this, please do so before the wedding. If there are any known triggers (like settings, sounds, touches, etc.), share them with your partner so you can be sensitive to each other and avoid them as much as possible.

6. Is there something that could affect your sex life that you need to seek help for before marriage? For instance, could you benefit from seeing a trauma therapist, going to a licensed counselor, or dealing with porn or other addictions? What plans do you have to adequately address any roadblocks before the wedding?

Planning for the Honeymoon/Wedding Night

7. Discuss your expectations for the wedding night. Are you both confident that you'll be able to go at the slower person's pace? How can you make sure that you aim for arousal on your honeymoon?

8. What is your main goal for your honeymoon? Do you want

to experience a big adventure together, or do you want something more relaxed? Do you want to travel or stay closer to home? If sex will be new for you, is what you're planning conducive to getting used to sex? Talk about how to plan for a honeymoon that will be the most memorable while also helping you feel intimate, relaxed, and comfortable.

Planning for Romance

9. How are you going to keep having fun outside the bedroom once you're married? What things are you doing now while you're dating that you want to make sure you continue?

10. Each of you think of a time when your beloved did something that showed that they loved and cherished you. What about it made you feel special? Share that memory. How can you each bring more romance into your relationship?

Planning for Sex

11. For many couples, orgasm is a skill that takes a while to learn. How will you handle it if orgasm is difficult for her? What will you do to both bring down the pressure and also keep aiming for her pleasure?

12. Turn to the diagram for the sexual response cycle (p. 27). Do you understand the difference between excitement, arousal, and orgasm? Reassure your partner that you will give her the time and attention needed to go through each stage.

13. One of the key factors in women's orgasm is women feeling they can speak up during sex if something isn't working for them. Discuss: what is the best way that you can make it easier for her to feel like she can speak up? Are there things that either of you are nervous about communicating during sex? How can you reassure each other that speaking up isn't a criticism, but a desire to move towards real passion?

Commit to each other now that you will speak up during sex when things aren't going the way you want, and that you will respond positively to your partner if that happens.

14. Did you grow up hearing that sex is a duty that people need to perform in marriage? Have you believed this? How will you ensure that in your marriage sex will always be something that is mutual and never coerced or pressured? Talk about how you will handle each other's "no."

15. Are there things you would like your spouse to do that you think will help you feel loved and close during sex? Discuss these together.

For Married Couples

This book comes with a companion book for your wife—*The Good Girl's Guide to Great Sex*! Ideally, have her read her book, and then, after you're both finished, set aside two or three blocks of time to discuss these questions together.

Setting the Stage

1. God made sex to be intimate, mutual, and pleasurable for both. In which area do you think you're strongest as a couple? Which area do you think you struggle with most? Think about it individually and then compare answers. Discuss ways you can improve the areas you both feel need improvement (especially if they're different!).

2. Is there an area of your sex life where you might benefit from some outside help (from a doctor, a pelvic floor physiotherapist, a licensed marriage counselor, a trauma-informed counselor, a porn recovery group). What have been the barriers to getting that help? How can you overcome them?

Emotional Intimacy

3. What kind of touch warms you up and makes you more interested in sex? Are there kinds of touch that make you less interested? What would you like your spouse to do more of?

4. Each of you think of a time when your spouse did something that showed that they loved and cherished you. What was about it made you feel special? Share that memory with your spouse. How can you each bring more romance into your relationship?

Physical Intimacy

5. Turn to the diagram for the sexual response cycle (p. 27). Are there steps you feel you may have been skipping or rushing through too quickly? Discuss ways to make sex feel as good as possible for both of you.

6. Are you both regularly reaching orgasm? If not, discuss how you will make the person who is not reaching orgasm a priority in your lovemaking. Are there certain positions or types of stimulation that are more likely to lead to orgasm? Women often feel self-conscious if orgasm takes too long or isn't happening. Is this a problem for you? If so, how will you address it? Men sometimes get defensive if they're asked to do different things in bed to stimulate her. Is this a problem for you? If so, how will you address it?

7. During a sexual encounter, do you each feel comfortable communicating with your spouse in the moment if something isn't working or you want something different? If not, identify the barriers that keep you from doing so. Is there something you or your spouse can do to make this easier?

Spiritual Intimacy

8. When you're making love, do you feel emotionally close to your spouse? How can you enhance your emotional connection during sex?

9. Share with your spouse your favorite sexual memory. What was it about that encounter that was so amazing? What can you do to create more sexual memories?

10. Are there things that would like to do to spice up the bedroom? Talk openly to each other about your ideas. Remember the principles in the book about how adding spice is meant to enhance intimacy, not detract from it, and honor each other's "no."

11. Do you feel comfortable stopping a sexual encounter if it's not working for you? How can you and your spouse set up a dynamic where both of you feel free to initiate or to stop things without any fear or guilt? Do you ever have sex only out of obligation? What can you each do to change this dynamic so that sex is something you each enter enthusiastically? (If coercion is ever a part of your sexual life, please seek help.)

Libido

12. What are your top three libido killers? Guess your spouse's and compare notes. What can you each do to reduce your spouse's libido killers?

13. Do you have a spontaneous or responsive libido? What do you think your spouse has? Compare answers. Of the two of you, does one of you want sex more? Does one want it less? How can you make sure you're making each other feel wanted and desired based on the principles in this book?

14. Out of the last five times you made love, who initiated: him, her, or both of you? Compare your answers. Are you happy with this, or do you want to make some changes?

Acknowledgments

We're so grateful to have such a wonderful team around us to bring *The Good Guy's Guide to Great Sex* to fruition. Sheila's been wanting to write this book for years, and we're thankful to Carolyn McCready at Zondervan for championing this project and especially for helping Sheila bring the dream of rewriting *The Good Girl's Guide to Great Sex* to life so we have two awesome companion books to share together. Chip MacGregor, our agent, is always ready to go to bat for us and tell us when an idea is really bad—or really good. We're glad he thought this one was really good.

We could not have written this book without the expertise and hard work of Joanna Sawatsky, our stats expert and dear friend. We're looking forward to all the peer-reviewed publications that she will one day write with this treasure trove of data! Speaking of data, a special thank you to the over three thousand men who took our survey. We know it was long. We appreciate your time and your trust in us to handle it well.

We also must acknowledge that, like most of Sheila's books and pretty much all her podcasts, the best lines tend to be from our daughter Rebecca Lindenbach. In fact, one of Kim Tanner's (our copy editor's) comments read: "This paragraph right here could be the whole book! You don't need anything else!" We looked at the paragraph, and sure enough, Rebecca had dictated it, almost word for word, on a walk that Sheila took with her and our grandson that morning. So thank you, Rebecca. We know it's weird that we talk about sex so much with you, but you're awesome. And you're way funnier and snarkier than we are.

And thank you, Kim, for all your hard work too, including wading through all the statistics! You took some of the confusing stuff and made it so much clearer. We appreciate it.

Thank you so much to our team on the *Bare Marriage* blog: our son-in-law Connor Lindenbach, who runs the technical side; our daughter Katie Emmerson, who edits the *Bare Marriage* podcast; our friend Emily Murchison, who helps with social media; and of course our friend Tammy Arseneau, who basically manages our lives. We appreciate you all so much. And to Elizabeth Wray, Sheila's mom who lives with us and tries to make our lives as easy as she can when we're in work mode—we see it and appreciate it, even if we don't say it often enough.

To my (Keith's) parents Ron and Cheryl Gregoire, who showed me what a long, loving, lasting marriage could look like: thank you.

We want to say a special shout-out to several people who have informed the way we think about male sexuality, especially Andrew J. Bauman and Michael John Cusick. They have so graciously shared their work and their thoughts with us, and we find it refreshing that there are Christian men writing in this sphere with a Jesus-centered approach to healing from sexual addictions and achieving wholeness. We also appreciate Emily Nagoski's work about the female sexual response cycle, which helped us use different words when we talk about libido.

Thank you to the team at FamilyLife Canada who first saw that I (Keith) had speaking potential and pushed me into the role of marriage speaker. Without their support, Sheila would still likely be doing this alone.

And finally, thank you to all our online social media followers and commenters who challenge us, help us hone our approach, and encourage us to keep going. Thank you especially to our male commenters who have become like friends and have shaped how we wrote this book from our years of interactions—Adam, Chris, Nathan, Chuck, Phil—and yes, even Doug.

To all our Bare Marriage Patreon supporters: it is wonderful to have you to run our ideas off of before we put them to paper. Thank you for cheering us on as we wrote for women and for championing us as we decided to write for men too.

Notes

Chapter 1: What Is Great Sex?

1. Sheila's blog has recently rebranded to *Bare Marriage*. From 2008–2021, it was *To Love, Honor and Vacuum*.
2. In the beginning of our marriage, Sheila suffered from vaginismus, an involuntary contraction of the muscles of the vaginal wall. We'll talk more about that later in the book, but please know that painful sex is not something you should put up with. Please seek out a pelvic floor physiotherapist or a physician to help you work through this.

Chapter 2: Let's Get Medical (How Sex Works)

1. Vincenzo Puppo and Ilan Gruenwald, "Does the G-Spot Exist? a Review of the Current Literature," *International Urogynecology Journal* 23 (June 2012): 1665–669, https://doi.org/10.1007/s00192 -012-1831-y. The reason that the region generally associated with the "G-spot" seems to be more pleasurable for women is likely related to the fact that when a woman has her pelvis tilted, other anatomical areas press against her vaginal wall, putting pressure on the upper vaginal wall. The general consensus today is that the clitoris has "roots" that extend upward, and these are stimulated when pressure is put on the front of the vaginal wall. This may also be why women who report having sex when they feel a slight need to urinate report higher degrees of pleasure—the bladder is pushing down in that direction.

2. Some women can also ejaculate at orgasm, but this is not necessary for orgasm.

3. If she experiences a great deal of pain at ovulation, see a physician.

4. For example, the Billings Ovulation Method: www.the billingsovulationmethod.org.

5. If life begins at conception, then a contraception method that allows conception but prevents implantation could be seen as violating the pro-life position. The scientific consensus seems to be, however, that this is not how hormonal methods work. Preventing ovulation, paired with increased cervical mucus that prevents sperm from entering the uterus, means conception doesn't occur.

6. Zlatko Pastor, Katerina Holla, and Roman Chmel, "The Influence of Combined Oral Contraceptives on Female Sexual Desire: A Systematic Review," *The European Journal of Contraception and Reproductive Health Care* 18, no. 1 (February 2013): 27–43, https://doi.org/10.3109/13625187.2012.728643.

7. *Study: Copper IUDs Do Not Appear to Prevent Implantation or Increase HIV Risk*, Relias Media, July 1, 2020, https://www.reliasmedia.com /articles/146320-study-copper-iuds-do-not-appear-to-prevent -implantation-or-increase-hiv-risk.

Chapter 3: Let's Get Frisky! The Sexual Response Cycle

1. There's no definitive description of the sexual arousal cycle in medical literature. Some include "libido" or "desire" instead of excitement; some include "plateau" instead of "arousal." Most use just four phases. We've decided to use these five phases, with the plateau phase in parentheses, since we think they describe women's sexuality the best, and that's what we want guys to understand.

2. With thanks to Emily Nagoski, *Come as You Are* (New York: Simon & Schuster, 2015), whose work helped us talk about different libidos in a more accessible way.

3. Ekaterina Mitricheva et al., "Neural Substrates of Sexual Arousal Are Not Sex Dependent," *Proceedings of the National Academy of Sciences* 116, no. 31 (July 2019): 15671–76, https://doi.org/10.1073 /pnas.1904975116.

Chapter 4: Mind the Gap!

1. For purposes of this statistic, we excluded men who suffered from erectile dysfunction, since intercourse and ejaculation were impacted by sexual dysfunction. When men suffering from erectile dysfunction are included, the number drops to 91.3%.

2. Interestingly, we found no difference in women's self-reported orgasm rates and their husband's estimates. So we can't claim ignorance, guys!

3. As the last graph shows, many women don't prioritize their own pleasure either. Indeed, 52.3 percent of women who infrequently orgasm still say their husbands do "enough" foreplay—which makes us wonder, enough for what?

4. See, for instance, Shaunti Feldhahn, *For Women Only* (Colorado Springs: Multnomah, 2004), 102–103, where she talks about how men don't enjoy sex unless their wives are into it, but she doesn't say that men should make sure that their wives feel pleasure. In fact, she says that if women don't feel pleasure, their priority should be to make sure their husband feels encouraged and wanted during the encounter.

5. Here's a quote from *Love & Respect*, which epitomizes this philosophy: "If your husband is typical, he has a need you don't have." Emerson Eggerichs, *Love & Respect: The Love She Most Desires, The Respect He Desperately Needs* (Nashville: Thomas Nelson, 2004) 258. Emerson Eggerichs insinuates that the typical man needs sex, while the typical woman doesn't. This attitude is prevalent in Christian sex and marriage books, as discussed in Sheila's book *The Great Sex Rescue*. If you and your wife have struggled to overcome bad teaching you had in the church about sex, it's a great resource.

Chapter 5: Going Back to Square One

1. See, for instance, Shaunti Feldhahn and Lisa A. Rice, *For Young Women Only* (Colorado Springs: Multnomah, 2006), 48, where they talk about how 82 percent of boys won't want to stop or be able to stop in a make-out situation, and so the girls will have to set the boundaries. For further discussion on how this affects women, see

Sheila's book *The Great Sex Rescue*, chapter 4. Rachel Joy Welcher's *Talking Back to Purity Culture* (InterVarsity Press, 2020) also discusses this at length.

2. This is likely why girls who believe that boys will want to push their sexual boundaries are 24 percent less likely to orgasm frequently in marriage and 28 percent less likely to be confident about their ability to get aroused during sexual activity—along with all kinds of other ill effects! For more information on the effect of this belief on women's sexuality, see *The Great Sex Rescue*, 66–67.

Chapter 6: Ladies First (All about Orgasm)

1. Gajanan S. Bhat and Anuradha Shastry, "Time to Orgasm in Women in a Monogamous Stable Heterosexual Relationship," *The Journal of Sexual Medicine* 17, no. 4 (2020): 749–60, https://doi .org/10.1016/j.jsxm.2020.01.005.

2. Marcel D. Waldinger et al., "A Multinational Population Survey of Intravaginal Ejaculation Latency Time," *Journal of Sexual Medicine* 2, no. 4 (July 2005): 492–97, https://doi.org/10.1111/j.1743-6109 .2005.00070.x.

3. David A. Frederick et al., "Differences in Orgasm Frequency Among Gay, Lesbian, Bisexual, and Heterosexual Men and Women in a U.S. National Sample," *Archives of Sexual Behavior* 47 (January 2018): 273–88, https://doi.org/10.1007/s10508-017-0939-z.

4. Frederick, "Differences in Orgasm Frequency."

5. For more information on how to do Kegels, see https://www .mayoclinic.org/diseases-conditions/premature-ejaculation /diagnosis-treatment/drc-20354905.

Chapter 7: When Sex Isn't Working

1. Eliana V. Carraca et al., "Body Image Change and Improved Eating Self-Regulation in a Weight Management Intervention for Women," *International Journal of Behavioral Nutrition and Physical Activity* 8, no. 75 (July 2011), https://doi.org/10.1186/1479-5868-8-75.

2. Some of the 6.8 percent of women for whom penetration was

impossible may have been suffering from postpartum pain rather than vaginismus; we didn't differentiate in that question.

3. Vaginal trainers are commonly called dilators, but many physiotherapists now refer to them as trainers because it's a less intimidating word.

4. Raymond C. Rosen et al., "Men's Attitudes to Life Events and Sexuality (Males) Study. The Multinational Men's Attitudes to Life Events and Sexuality (Males) Study: I. Prevalence of Erectile Dysfunction and Related Health Concerns in the General Population," *Current Medical Research and Opinion* 20, no. 5 (May 2004): 607–17, https://doi.org/10.1185/030079904125003467.

5. Ahmed Adam et al., "Is the History of Erectile Dysfunction a Reliable Risk Factor for New Onset Acute Myocardial Infarction? A Systematic Review and Meta-Analysis," *Current Urology* 14 (October 2020): 122–129, https://doi.org/10.1159/000499249.

6. For more information, see https://www.urologyhealth.org/urology -a-z/p/premature-ejaculation.

Chapter 8: The Greatest Need

1. John Gottman, "Building a Great Sex Life Is Not Rocket Science," The Gottman Institute, January 4, 2017, https://www.gottman.com /blog/building-great-sex-life-not-rocket-science/.

2. Justin J. Lehmiller, "How the Most Satisfied Couples Maintain Their Passion: An Interview with the Gottmans on Maintaining a Healthy Sex Life," *Psychology Today*, March 4, 2019, https://www .psychologytoday.com/us/blog/the-myths-sex/201903/how-the -most-satisfied-couples-maintain-their-passion.

3. John Powell, *Why Am I Afraid to Tell You Who I Am?* (Grand Rapids: Zondervan, 1999).

Chapter 9: Sex Sorta Begins in the Kitchen (But Not Why You Think)

1. Allison Daminger, "The Cognitive Dimension of Household Labor," *American Sociological Review* 84, no. 4 (July 9, 2019): 609–33, https://doi.org/10.1177/0003122419859007.

2. Patricia Hirsch, Iring Koch, and Julia Karbach, "Putting a Stereotype to the Test: The Case of Gender Differences in Multitasking Costs in Task-Switching and Dual-Task Situations," *PLoS ONE* 14, no. 8: e0220150, https://doi.org/10.1371/journal.pone.0220150.

3. American Academy of Pediatrics, "Infant Sleep Safety Overview," https://www.aap.org/en/patient-care/safe-sleep/, and Canadian Pediatric Society and the Government of Canada, "Joint Statement of Safe Sleep," https://www.canada.ca/en/public-health/services/health-promotion/childhood-adolescence/stages-childhood/infancy-birth-two-years/safe-sleep/joint-statement-on-safe-sleep.html.

Chapter 10: Let's Get Romantic

1. Sheila Wray Gregoire, *31 Days to Great Sex* (Grand Rapids: Zondervan, 2020), 80–84.

Chapter 11: Making Love, Not Just Having Sex

1. Lucy Fry, "Intimacy and Space," The Gottman Institute, May 12, 2020, https://www.gottman.com/blog/intimacy-and-space/.

2. Fry, "Intimacy and Space."

3. Andrew J. Bauman, *The Sexually Healthy Man: Essays on Spirituality, Sexuality & Restoration* (self-pub., 2021), 105.

4. John Donne, *John Donne: The Major Works* (Oxford: Oxford University Press, 2000), 177.

5. Bauman, *The Sexually Healthy Man*, 102.

Chapter 12: When Sex Seems Ugly

1. National Sexual Violence Resource Center, "Statistics," https://www.nsvrc.org/statistics.

2. Bessel van der Kolk, *The Body Keeps the Score: Brain, Mind, and Body in the Healing of Trauma* (New York: Penguin: 2015), 80. We are aware that Bessel van der Kolk himself has been credibly accused of harassing those who worked with him, and we are sad about this. However, his book contains so much great truth that we want to

quote from it. We're sad that someone with this much insight could act that way in his personal life.

3. Van der Kolk, *The Body Keeps the Score*, 92.

4. Personal email with Rachael Denhollander, from September 4, 2020, used with permission.

Chapter 13: Is Sex a Need?

1. The confidence intervals for the increased incidence of sexual pain from believing the obligation sex message before marriage and from prior abuse were separated by 0.1 percent. This indicates that while there is a statistically significant difference between the rate of vaginismus associated with prior abuse and the rate of vaginismus associated with believing the obligation sex message, this difference is very small. Because abuse is such a well-established (and profoundly understandable) cause of vaginismus, the association of obligation sex and vaginismus is, we believe, very noteworthy.

2. Sheila Wray Gregoire, Rebecca Gregoire Lindenbach, and Joanna Sawatsky, *The Great Sex Rescue* (Grand Rapids: Baker, 2021), 173.

3. "The most difficult time for this man was during his wife's period, because she was unavailable to him sexually. After about ten years, she finally realized that pleasing her husband with oral sex or a simple 'hand job' did wonders to help her husband through that difficult time. She realized that faithfulness is a two-person job. That doesn't mean a husband can escape the blame for using pornography by pointing to an uncooperative wife—we all make our own choices—but a wife can make it much easier for her husband to maintain a pure mind." Dr. Kevin Leman, *Sheet Music: Uncovering the Secrets of Sexual Intimacy in Marriage* (Carol Stream, IL: Tyndale, 2008), 49.

4. Blake Bakkila, "This Is How Many Women Actually Have Period Sex," Health.com, April 13, 2018, https://www.health.com /condition/sexual-health/how-many-woman-have-period-sex.

5. Leviticus 15:19 says, "When a woman has her regular flow of blood, the impurity of her monthly period will last seven days, and anyone who touches her will be unclean till evening." Periods average three to seven days, so most are shorter than the full seven days

prescribed here. Some Jewish traditions apply Leviticus 15:28 to her period as well: "When she is cleansed from her discharge, she must count off seven days, and after that she will be ceremonially clean." She was not clean again until seven days after the last day of her period, for a total of fourteen days.

6. Leviticus 12:2–5.

7. Sheila's own books were excluded from the study to avoid bias, but all of Sheila's books on sex do mention consent, including *The Good Girl's Guide to Great Sex*, *31 Days to Great Sex*, and *The Great Sex Rescue*. Of the books that *The Great Sex Rescue* studied, *Boundaries in Marriage* covered consent in general well, though it didn't give a robust definition of consent in the bedroom (but that was also not its main topic). *The Gift of Sex* also handled the topic fairly well but didn't go over all the different forms of coercion.

8. See, for example, the story of Aunt Matilda in Tim and Beverly LaHaye, *The Act of Marriage: The Beauty of Sexual Love* (Grand Rapids: Zondervan, 1998), 107. Tim LaHaye tells the story of Aunt Matilda, who warned her engaged niece about the perils of sex and how awful it was. LaHaye explains how Aunt Matilda's husband had raped her, while she kicked and screamed, on her wedding night, and had continued to rape her throughout her marriage, so Aunt Matilda had a very bad view of sex. LaHaye's point in this story was very misplaced, to put it mildly: Isn't it terrible of Aunt Matilda to distort her niece's expectations of sex? And he called Matilda's husband "equally unhappy" as the wife he had repeatedly raped his whole marriage.

9. Having sexual pleasure or a sexual response does not mean the encounter was consensual. "Arousal nonconcordance" is the phenomenon where your body and brain are not aligned with each other. One's body can become aroused and even reach orgasm even if the brain is telling you that you don't want this.

Chapter 14: You Don't Need That Fix

1. See, for example, Timothy Head, "Porn Consumption Is Contributing to Child Sex Trafficking Epidemic," *The Hill*, March 2,

2018, https://thehill.com/opinion/criminal-justice/376500-porn
-consumption-is-contributing-to-child-sex-trafficking-epidemic.

2. The numbers in the graph add to 82.5 percent due to rounding. The
number without the rounding is 82.4 percent.

3. See, for example, Barbara A. Steffens and Robyn L. Rennie, "The
Traumatic Nature of Disclosure for Wives of Sexual Addicts," *Sexual
Addiction & Compulsivity* 13 (2006): 247–67, https://doi.org/10.1080
/10720160600870802.

4. Stephen Arterburn and Fred Stoeker, *Every Man's Battle: Winning the
War on Sexual Temptation One Victory at a Time* (Colorado Springs:
Waterbrook, 2000), 118.

5. Michael John Cusick, *Surfing for God: Discovering the Divine Design
Beneath Sexual Struggle* (Nashville: Nelson, 2012), 17.

6. Cusick, *Surfing for God*, 59–60.

7. Bauman, *Sexually Healthy Man*, 53.

8. In fact, 23.18 percent do use porn in regular or intermittent binges,
but not all consider themselves as having a problem with porn now.

9. Cusick, *Surfing for God*, xv.

10. Cusick, *Surfing for God*, xvi.

11. Cusick, *Surfing for God*, 80.

12. Cusick, *Surfing for God*, 80.

Chapter 15: Beyond Bouncing Your Eyes

1. We included this particular scenario because the iconic evangelical
book on lust—Stephen Arterburn and Fred Stoeker, *Every Man's
Battle: Winning the War on Sexual Temptation One Victory at a Time*
(Colorado Springs: Waterbrook, 2000)—presented it as if it were a
normal occurrence (p. 13). So we wanted to test this scenario. Do
men struggle with not lusting after young moms pulling toddlers
out of car seats? Turns out, no, they don't. (Which is what we
hypothesized in the first place.)

2. Much of the discourse around the problem with men's lust has been
fueled in the evangelical world by Shaunti Feldhahn's surveys about
men and lust. Specifically, she measured what she termed a "mental
rolodex" and later updated to "mental photo file of sensual images."

For Women Only (Colorado Springs: Multnomah, 2013), 136. Her survey found that only 13 percent of men reported they didn't have such a mental file (p. 138). However, her survey question did not distinguish whether these images actually were plaguing people or whether they simply had memories. We wanted to phrase the question in a way that clarified whether or not men experienced their memories as problems. Overall, 41.8 percent of men said they were frequently tempted to lust by past images, and with 52.9 percent of men who said they struggled with lust on a daily basis answering in the affirmative. We believe that portraying lust as an ongoing, constant problem for all men is not warranted from the research and does not help men fight lust.

3. Arterburn and Stoeker, *Every Man's Battle*, 125.
4. For more findings on how the fear that men will lust affects women's marital and sexual satisfaction outcomes, see chapter 5 of *The Great Sex Rescue*.
5. Paige Patterson in "Paige Patterson Objectifies a 16 Year Old Girl," Baptistblogger, May 6, 2018, YouTube video, 1:54, https://www .youtube.com/watch?v=gDRUVmcaQ3k&t=11s.

Chapter 16: Adding Some Spice

1. Sheila Wray Gregoire, *31 Days to Great Sex* (Grand Rapids: Zondervan, 2020), 165.
2. Wray Gregoire, *31 Days to Great Sex*, 165–66.

Chapter 17: When You Want More

1. Elizabeth A. Schoenfeld et al., "Does Sex Really Matter? Examining the Connections Between Spouses' Nonsexual Behaviors, Sexual Frequency, Sexual Satisfaction, and Marital Satisfaction," *Archives of Sexual Behavior* 46, no. 2 (February 2017): 489–501, https://doi.org /10.1007/s10508-015-0672-4.
2. Sheila Wray Gregoire, Rebecca Gregoire Lindenbach, and Joanna Sawatsky, *The Great Sex Rescue: The Lies You've Been Taught and How to Recover What God Intended* (Grand Rapids: Baker, 2021), 133.
3. Markham Heid, "Here's How Much Sex You Should Have Every

Week," *Time*, March 7, 2017, https://time.com/4692326/how
-much-sex-is-healthy-in-a-relationship/.

4. Andrew Bauman, "I Deserve Sex: Addressing Entitlement
   over Women's Bodies," Andrew J. Bauman, February 19, 2020,
   https://andrewjbauman.com/i-deserve-sex/.

5. We want to say, too, that this is indicative of an emotionally and
   sexually abusive relationship. If you treat your wife badly if she
   does not have sex with you, then you are creating a fear-based
   marriage. Make sure your wife feels safe, and see a licensed
   counselor if you recognize yourself in this scenario.

Appendix 1: Getting Ready for the Honeymoon

1. The book was *The Act of Marriage* by Tim and Beverly LaHaye. For
   more information on the effects of this sort of advice on newlyweds,
   see Sheila's book *The Great Sex Rescue*.

2. For this statistic, we controlled for prior abuse, so that was not a
   confounding factor. We compared women who had had sex for
   the first time after the wedding with those who had had sex before
   the wedding, but only with the person they were now married to.
   Vaginismus rates were lower if sex had occurred before marriage.

3. For instance, women who believe the "obligation sex" message—
   that they must have sex when their husbands want it—are 39
   percent more likely to suffer from vaginismus. When women feel
   as if sex is not something they freely choose, their bodies often
   rebel, almost in a trauma-like response. This is not conscious, and
   a woman can't just turn it off. Instead, work at helping her feel
   safe and helping her have agency over her body, and then seek out
   pelvic floor therapy treatment if it continues.

The Good Girl's Guide to Great Sex

Creating a Marriage That's Both Holy and Hot

Sheila Wray Gregoire

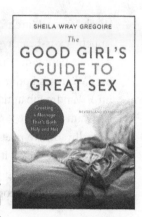

Bring greater satisfaction to your relationship in every way—emotionally, spiritually, and physically—whether you're preparing for your honeymoon or are empty nesters looking for a new spark.

Are you wondering if there's more to your sex life than the status quo? Or maybe you have questions about your upcoming marriage that aren't exactly appropriate for the rehearsal dinner? This edition of *The Good Girl's Guide to Great Sex* from tell-it-like-it-is blogger and speaker Sheila Wray Gregoire has been completely updated and expanded to include new research from surveys of more than twenty-five thousand people. With humor, stories, and highly practical ideas, Sheila helps you:

- See how God intends sex to unite couples physically, emotionally, and spiritually—and how to overcome roadblocks in each area
- Understand more about your two bodies and how they were meant to go together
- Find healing from past sexual experiences, sexual trauma, or pornography addiction
- Figure out the missing piece in your sex life that often makes pleasure out of reach
- Learn how to help your husband give you greater pleasure than ever before
- Embrace sex with freedom, rather than viewing it with shame or embarrassment

Available in stores and online!